BT
3.25

# Eisenhower, Brownell, and the Congress

## *The Tangled Origins of the Civil Rights Bill of 1956-1957*

J. W. ANDERSON

# Eisenhower, Brownell, and the Congress

*The Tangled Origins of the Civil Rights Bill of 1956-1957*

*Published for*

THE INTER-UNIVERSITY
CASE PROGRAM

*by*

UNIVERSITY OF ALABAMA PRESS

*University, Alabama*

*This is Case Study 80*
*in the Inter-University Case Program Series*

# Contents

# Preface

MR. ANDERSON's study was commissioned by The Inter-University Case Program as one of a group of case studies designed to shed light on the dynamics of Congressional policy-making. Mr. Anderson and other case writers in the Congressional case series have been encouraged to depart, where necessary, from the case study forms commonly used in the ICP cases that deal primarily with the workings of the executive branch. They have been encouraged also to use broad perspectives in their research and writing to do justice to all the forces and factors that seem to them to influence the formation of national policies by the Congress, including influences arising outside of the legislative branch.

Mr. Anderson's original mission was the preparation of a study of the passage of the Civil Rights Act of 1957. His research convinced him that the passage of the Act in 1957 could not be meaningfully understood without a detailed knowledge of the unsuccessful efforts to pass similar legislation in 1956. The present case deals entirely with the 1956 legislative effort.

Mr. Anderson was granted a Congressional Fellowship in 1956 by the American Political Science Association, and has been attempting to reconstruct the history of the Civil Rights Act of 1957 ever since. He is an editorial writer for the *Washington Post*.

This study was made possible by a grant from the Ford Foundation and by support from the more than seventy universities that participate in the work of The Inter-University

Case Program. A non-profit corporation, the ICP fosters the preparation of case studies of the actual workings of the governmental process in the United States and abroad. It operates under the direction of an inter-university Board of Trustees, and its central office is located on the campus of the Maxwell Graduate School, Syracuse University, 607 University Avenue, Syracuse, N.Y.

EDWIN A. BOCK
*President, Inter-University Case Program, Inc.*
*Professor of Political Science, Syracuse University*

# Eisenhower, Brownell, and the Congress

*The Tangled Origins of the Civil Rights Bill
of 1956-1957*

# ( I )

# The Justice Department Drafts a Civil Rights Program

THREE DAYS AFTER CHRISTMAS OF 1955, At-
torney General Herbert Brownell directed the Justice Department's technicians to begin drafting a civil rights bill. That
date was the turning point in the Eisenhower administration's policy toward the most divisive issue in contemporary
American politics.

When the Republican administration first took office, nearly
three years before, the Senate Majority Leader, Robert A.
Taft of Ohio, privately warned the newcomers to Washington
that the passage of new civil rights legislation was a hopeless
cause. President Truman had tried it, and he had been beaten
in a long and savage struggle in the Senate. In their eagerness
to set the federal government on a new and more profitable
course, the Eisenhower men had little interest in spending their
energy blowing on the embers of their predecessors' disasters.
At the Cabinet level, the incoming Republicans tacitly ratified
their party's old compact with the Southern Democrats.
Farther down in the Justice Department, the officials specifically charged with administration of the federal civil rights
laws approached gingerly a field that was notoriously difficult
legally as well as politically. The chief responsibility here lay

with Warren Olney III, Assistant Attorney General for the Criminal Division. He took time to accustom himself to the peculiarities of civil rights law, and then, with a good deal of force but not much publicity, he began operating in the area of the most indisputably direct federal jurisdiction. When the Supreme Court held in 1954 (*Brown* vs. *Board of Education*) that segregated public schools were unconstitutional, the President promptly told the District of Columbia Commissioners to integrate Washington's two school systems.

But the Supreme Court's school decision gave new heat to the old debate over Negroes' rights. After a few months of stunned silence, many Southern political figures began to declare, with growing determination, that they would not submit to the decision. Who, then, was to enforce it, and how? In Hoxie, Arkansas the school board admitted some Negro children to white classrooms in the fall of 1955 and was immediately subjected to a campaign of harassment by organized segregationists. At one point that year a boycott forced the schools to close altogether. And behind the Hoxie case lay the much more prevalent instances of school boards receiving explicit instructions from governors and legislatures not to attempt desegregation even in areas (like northern Virginia) where local opinion was not wholly unreceptive to it.

The school decision generated a public interest in Negroes' rights unprecedented since Reconstruction. It carried the issue into every village of the South, and there the knowledge of a great victory for the Negro generated among many white men a renewed determination to resist. For some years Southern Negroes had generally found increasing success in their attempts to register and vote. Suddenly, after the school decision, Negroes in several states found themselves the object of systematic disfranchisement drives, usually inspired by the White Citizens Councils. There was violence. In early August 1955 a Negro leader of a registration movement was shot and killed on the lawn of the Lincoln County, Mississippi, courthouse; no federal law had been violated, and state authorities never prosecuted although there had apparently been a crowd of witnesses. Two weeks later Emmett Till, a fourteen-year-old Negro boy from Chicago, on a visit to Mississippi, whistled at a white woman. His body was found shortly afterward, floating face down, in the Tallahatchie River. The identities of the murderers were apparently no secret locally. A public outcry arose, and Northern politicians demanded that the Justice Department step in. But again no federal law had been violated, and the state prosecutors showed a lack of energy; there were two state trials, neither of which resulted in conviction.

A resonance developed between South and North, and each new example of intransigence in the South was met with a new cry of outrage, particularly from those Northern cities with large Negro populations. The Southerners' open defiance of the Supreme Court gave an unprecedented dramatic focus to the Negroes' demands for legal equality.

Truman in 1948 and Eisenhower in 1952 had demonstrated in two different ways that support in Northern industrial cities was indispensable for winning a presidential election, but support from the South was not. In 1955 Eisenhower's party was thinking about the coming election, and there were Republicans, particularly congressmen from urban constituencies, who began to press the administration to take a forceful position on civil rights. In the Justice Department, Attorney General Herbert Brownell was sympathetic but remained unable to march into battle without orders from his chief. The orders were not forthcoming. Eisenhower commanded an enormous personal popularity that proved to be impervious to any of the usual political issues. As long as he was the party's candidate, it was virtually certain that the party could win the Presidency again. The Republicans interested in civil rights as a matter of principle appeared to be in the minority, and in the absence of any compelling partisan or tactical necessity for involving the party in that controversial issue, most of the party leaders were unwilling to take the risks.

All of that changed immediately when Eisenhower suffered a heart attack in late September 1955. He was in a hospital bed until early November and convalescent for another two months. In that time his Cabinet and staff carried on the work of the Presidency, while politicians and newspapers wondered about the 1956 presidential election only a year away. As time passed, it seemed doubtful that the President would run for a second term; if he were to run, the effect of his illness on voters would be incalculable. The Republican administration now became responsive to all the pressures that normally affect politicians at the beginning of election campaigns.

Brownell went quietly about the delicate work of obtaining presidential consent for an administration civil rights bill. He could not invoke the support of congressmen or liberal organizations; he could hardly attempt to pressure a sick President. But he was able to bring the subject up within the Cabinet. It was discussed there only in the most general terms, but in these general terms the Cabinet consented to let Brownell proceed with the preparation of a civil rights bill. According to this understanding, the bill should go to Congress over Brownell's own name instead of the President's. By that small measure, at least, the temporary managers of the White House intended the President to remain detached from a project for which they knew him to have not much enthusiasm. The President ratified the Cabinet's decision and agreed to touch the subject in his State of the Union Message. It was on the basis of this assent that Brownell directed his Justice Department's Civil Rights Section, at the end of December, to begin drafting the program.

The President's Message was read to Congress on January 5. Eisenhower was recuperating in Key West, still not able to return to his desk in Washington. Toward the bottom of the long speech were three paragraphs on civil rights.

"We are proud of the progress our people have made in the

field of civil rights," Eisenhower said.[1] "In Executive Branch operations throughout the nation, elimination of discrimination and segregation is all but completed." He cited improvements in government contractors' hiring and Armed Forces promotions, as well as the diminishing of racial restrictions in Washington's hotels, restaurants, and theaters.

"It is disturbing that in some localities allegations persist that Negro citizens are being deprived of their right to vote and are likewise being subjected to unwarranted economic pressures," the Message continued. Eisenhower recommended that a bipartisan commission examine "these charges."

"We must strive to have every person judged and measured by what he is, rather than by his color, race, or religion," he declared. Then came the essential sentence: "There will soon be recommended to the Congress a program further to advance the efforts of the Government, within the area of Federal responsibility, to accomplish these objectives." Neither the objectives nor, more important, the area of federal responsibility was defined.

These vague paragraphs reflected accurately the equally vague agreement within the Cabinet. The President himself gave no great emphasis to the matter. In Florida he recorded a brief version of the speech for television, and it did not include the reference to civil rights. He was chiefly concerned with the world's balance of military power, with the search for disarmament (nuclear and otherwise), with the balancing of the budget, and with a list of improvements in agriculture and welfare legislation.

Brownell at last had the President on record in favor of an administration civil rights bill. The question now was: what sort of bill?

From the beginning, the Attorney General made it clear to his staff that he wanted a forceful and effective bill. He sug-

[1] *Public Papers of the Presidents of the United States: Dwight D. Eisenhower: 1956* (Washington: U.S. GPO, 1958) (hereafter *Presidential Papers*), p. 25.

gested that the draftsmen prepare, along with their other proposals, an anti-lynching bill. Always highly inflammatory to Southern political spokesmen, anti-lynching bills presumed the failure of the states to enforce their own criminal laws. Such a bill therefore represented the widest possible definition of the federal responsibility.

But the Department's civil rights specialists knew exactly what they needed from Congress and worked rapidly. In the sixteen years since it had been established, the Civil Rights Section in the Criminal Division of the Department of Justice had accumulated considerable experience with the meager and eccentric statutes provided on the subject by the U.S. Code.

## The Legal Background

The development of American civil rights law had always involved two quite separate problems. First was the definition of the American citizen's rights; then, enforcement of them.

The Justice Department's draftsmen were technicians and enforcement officers, not politicians. The bills over which Congress had fought since the New Deal had generally been devised by politicians and involved the dramatic business of creating new federal rights: a right to vote without being taxed for it, a right to be employed without racial distinction, an explicit right not to be lynched. But the enforcement officers were extremely anxious to obtain the statutory tools to effect the rights already declared by the courts—from the earliest, the right to vote, to the most recent, the right of access to public education without racial distinction.

Civil rights was one of the most complex fields in American law.[2] One cause of confusion was the degree to which

[2] See Robert K. Carr, *Federal Protection of Civil Rights: Quest for a Sword* (Ithaca: Cornell University Press, 1947) and Thomas I. Emerson and David Haber, *Political and Civil Rights in the United States* (2 vols., 2d ed., Buffalo, 1958). The latter contains an extensive bibliography. This chapter is indebted to both books.

historical accident and legislative neglect had fashioned the statutes. Another was the seventy years of congressional stalemate that had left the courts to grapple (in the infrequent cases that reached the appeal level) with the peculiarities of the original language. But, far more profound than these technical difficulties, the great political issue of states' rights was intertwined with the enforcement of individuals' rights. Federal and state responsibilities had always overlapped to some degree, even in matters most clearly within the traditional authority of the states. But the limits on this federal responsibility had always been in flux, and never more so than in the 1950's. Federal civil rights cases nearly always bore directly on this conflict. The violation of a federal right commonly grew out of events that also constituted a crime under state law for which state authorities were unable or unwilling to punish. In the racial segregation of school children, the federal violation was even enforced by state sanctions, and the collision of authorities the more rending.

Between 1866 and 1875, Congress passed seven acts to give force to the Thirteenth, Fourteenth, and Fifteenth Amendments. Over the next thirty years most of this law was either repealed by Congress or voided by the courts. It suffered further erosion in the 1909 codification. The only criminal statutes to survive, other than a peonage law, were the fragments carried in 1955 as Sections 241, 242, and 243 of the United States Code, Title 18.

Under Section 241 it was a felony to conspire to deprive a person of "any right or privilege" granted by the federal laws and Constitution. Section 242 made it a misdemeanor to deprive a person, "under color of any law," of his federally-secured rights. Section 243 prohibited racial discrimination in the selection of jurors, a statute that was successfully evaded in some counties by drawing juries from voter registration lists.

Some of the civil sections of the original Enforcement Acts also remained in effect, enabling a private individual to bring suit for damages or injunctive relief against any person depriving him of rights federally secured.

From the end of Reconstruction until the 1930's, these modest provisions were rarely used. The federal courts held to the narrowest constructions of existing law, Congress showed little inclination to provide new law, and the succession of attorneys general showed a corresponding disinterest in the manifest difficulties in using what meager powers remained. Without challenge many states, particularly in the South, developed formidable legal apparatus to enforce segregation.

But in 1939 Attorney General Frank Murphy established the Civil Rights Section in the Justice Department, and the volume of federal prosecutions rose rapidly. Over the next two decades most of the federal enforcement program was hinged upon two criminal statutes.[3] Section 241 was used most commonly to enforce other statutes establishing rights but carrying no sanctions. Section 242 was invoked principally in cases involving deprivation of liberty.

As basic authority for the entire federal civil rights program, these two statutes had limitations obvious from the beginning. Section 241 was a conspiracy law, and the prosecution had to prove, not that the defendant violated another citizen's federal rights, but, quite a different matter, that he had conspired with other people to violate them. Section 242 was a misdemeanor statute, carrying a maximum prison sentence of only one year.

More damaging still to the government's purpose, as the Civil Rights Section's activity began (in the 1940's) to generate tests of the statutes, a series of Supreme Court decisions demonstrated their less apparent shortcomings.

The *Screws* case[4] in 1945 put a particularly heavy burden

[3] A. B. Caldwell, "The Civil Rights Section: Its Functions and Its Statutes," an address reprinted in U.S. Cong., Senate, Subcommittee on Constitutional Rights, *Hearings, Civil Rights*, 85th Cong., 1st Sess., 1957, pp. 222-236.
[4] *Screws* v. *U.S.*, 325 U.S. 91.

on the prosecutors of rights violations under Section 242. Screws, Sheriff of Baker County, Georgia had arrested one Robert Hall on a charge of stealing a tire. With a policeman and a special deputy, Screws took Hall from his home late at night. Halting outside the jail, the three officers began beating the handcuffed prisoner with their fists and a blackjack. "Hall was then dragged feet first through the court house yard into the jail and thrown upon the floor dying."[5] There was evidence of a grudge between Screws and the dead man.

The Court's opinion, written by Justice William O. Douglas, condemned the crime but held that the jury had not been properly instructed. Only a narrow reading of Section 242 could prevent it from being voided entirely as unconstitutional, Douglas said.

The value of the two criminal statutes to the government lay precisely in their application to the full range of federal rights. But the *Screws* decision held that this useful breadth was achieved through a dangerous vagueness of language, enabling the Civil Rights Section to define a right by bringing a prosecution and to seek affirmation of it by the courts in subsequent appeals. In the Court's view, this procedure bore an unhealthy resemblance to writing law after the fact.

The question in *Screws* was whether the statute could properly prohibit violation by police officers of individuals' federally-secured rights where the extent of these rights was not explicit.

"Those who enforced local law today might not know for many months (and meanwhile could not find out) whether what they did deprived someone of due process of law," Douglas wrote. ". . . The constitutional vice of such a statute is the essential injustice to the accused of placing him on trial for an offence, the nature of which the statute does not define and hence of which it gives no warning." The Court ordered a new trial for the Sheriff, saying, in effect, that convictions

[5] *Idem.*

could be obtained under this vague statute only by clearly alleging and proving the defendant's intent to deprive a person of a specifically defined right. Screws, upon retrial, was acquitted and later became a state senator.

The division of the Court reflected the cloudiness of the issue. Only three of the other judges agreed with Douglas. Three judges wrote one dissent, a fourth wrote another. Justice Wiley Rutledge cast the decisive vote by concurring with Douglas. He would have preferred to affirm Screws' conviction, he explained, but that would have left the Court without a majority to dispose of the case.

The point was amplified by the Court in 1951 in *Williams* v. *United States*.[6] Williams, a private detective and special police officer in Miami, was hired by a lumber company to investigate a series of thefts. With the assistance of a policeman, he extracted confessions from four suspects through physical torture. The Court upheld his conviction under Section 242, and Justice Douglas once again wrote the opinion. ". . . When officers wring confessions from the accused by force and violence, they violate some of the most fundamental, basic and well-established constitutional rights which every citizen enjoys," he declared. The right to be free of coercion under questioning is clearly stated in the Constitution. And yet even in this case four justices dissented, three of them citing *Screws*.

In a companion case,[7] the Court was also asked whether Williams could be prosecuted under Section 241. He could not, the Court replied. The opinion was written by Justice Felix Frankfurter, a dissenter in both *Screws* and the other *Williams* case. Section 241 did not reach this kind of violation, Frankfurter argued, for it applied only to "interference with rights which arise from the relation of the victim and the Federal Government." The statute clearly applied to the right to vote, for example. But it did not apply to rights

[6] *Williams* v. *U.S.*, 341 U.S. 97 (1951).
[7] *U.S.* v. *Williams*, 341 U.S. 70 (1951).

"which the Constitution merely guarantees from interference by a state." Again the Court was split. Three justices joined Frankfurter, a fifth concurred, and four dissented. The diversity of opinion within the Court reflected the unsettled state of legal opinion generally on the constitutional concepts around which these cases turned.

The courts' handling of the parallel *civil* statutes was hardly more encouraging to those who were seeking general enforcement powers. Sections 1983 and 1985 of Title 42 were civil counterparts to Section 242 and 241 of Title 18, although the civil statutes were even narrower. Section 1971 of Title 42 authorized, in addition, suits by citizens whose voting rights were violated.

Before 1939, actions brought under these civil statutes were rare, mainly because victims of civil rights violations were seldom in a position to bring suit against their antagonists, commonly public officials. But in the 1940's an increasing number of cases invoked Section 1983. Most of them were thrown out of court, as judges hewed to narrow readings of the rights protected and to broad views on the immunities of public officials.[8] Section 1985 continued to be cited rarely.[9]

The most substantial advances were won, not in the cases involving the old Reconstruction statutes, but rather in the equity suits based directly on the Fourteenth and Fifteenth Amendments. In 1944, after seventeen years of litigation, the Supreme Court ruled the white primary illegal.[10] Ten years later the Court culminated another long series of cases with its unanimous decision in the *Brown* case that racially segregated schools constituted a violation of the Fourteenth Amendment,[11] perhaps the most significant legal victory of all for the Southern Negro. But these triumphs had more to do with the definition of federally-protected rights than with enforcement of them.

[8] Emerson and Haber, p. 82.          [9] *Ibid.,* p. 90.
[10] *Smith* v. *Allwright,* 321 U.S. 649.
[11] *Brown* v. *Board of Education,* 347 U.S. 483.

## Truman's Commission of 1946-1947

As a first step toward guaranteeing civil rights more effectively, President Truman had established in 1946 a Committee on Civil Rights headed by Charles E. Wilson, president of the General Electric company, to carry out a comprehensive survey of the problem. Truman said, "We must provide the Department of Justice with the tools to do the job."[12]

The Committee's recommendations in 1947 outlined virtually every major proposal that would appear in Congress for the next decade, including every section of the Civil Rights Act of 1957. Its report, "To Secure These Rights," was a compendium of all the cures that federal law might provide to all the wrongs the Committee's diligence had catalogued. Its suggestions varied widely in forcefulness. Some were mild, like the proposal for another commission to provide further study. Some were strong medicine, like the device (subsequently advocated by Representative Adam Clayton Powell) of conditioning all federal aid "to public or private agencies for any purpose" on the elimination of racial discrimination in their operations.[13] The report was lawyers' work. It viewed the realization of civil rights enforcement as essentially a question of law and administration rather than politics and economics. But it was the federal government's first thorough assessment of its responsibilities and a measure of the administration's increasing interest in them.

In his 1948 State of the Union Message, President Truman spoke of the need to "secure fully our essential human rights." A month later he proposed a broad program of legislation, declaring, ". . . there still are examples—flagrant examples —of discrimination which are utterly contrary to our

[12] President's Committee on Civil Rights, *To Secure These Rights* (Washington: U.S. G.P.O., 1947), p. vii.
[13] *Ibid.*, p. 166.

ideals."[14] He urged strengthening the criminal statutes, providing federal protection against lynching, insuring the right to vote, establishing a Fair Employment Practices Commission, and prohibiting discrimination in interstate transportation. He asked Congress to set up a Joint Committee on Civil Rights, a permanent Civil Rights Commission in the executive branch, and a Civil Rights Division in the Justice Department. He also asked the ballot for the disfranchised District of Columbia, statehood for Hawaii and Alaska, abolition of discriminatory naturalization restrictions, and fair settlement of losses claimed by Japanese-Americans evacuated to internment camps in World War II.

This program was launched in an election year, an accident that befell all administration civil rights bills over the next twelve years. Congress took no action. But after a dramatic fight the 1948 Democratic convention promised in its platform the enactment of civil rights legislation. In late April 1949 the Truman program was presented to Congress by Senator J. Howard McGrath of Rhode Island, then Chairman of the Democratic National Committee, formerly Truman's Solicitor General and later that year to become his Attorney General. In spite of such substantial sponsorship the program got nowhere.

The noisiest civil rights debate since the New Deal broke out the following year. From 1933 through 1950, only thirteen civil rights bills had generated enough political impetus to reach the Senate's calendar. All of them had been directed toward the federal punishment of lynching, the abolition of the poll tax, or the establishment of a federal Fair Employment Practices Commission.[15] In every case, when their other

[14] *Message of the President of the United States Transmitting His Recommendations for a Civil Rights Program* (Washington: U.S. GPO, 1948), Feb. 2, 1948.
[15] Tabulation prepared for Senator William F. Knowland by the Legislative Reference Service, *Congressional Record*, 85th Cong., 1st Sess., pp. 13893-13894.

parliamentary defenses were overcome, the Southern senators had succeeded in talking the bills to death. The most spectacular of these filibusters defeated the 1950 fair employment bill in a long and bitter session. To Northern Democrats, the defeat meant a step backward for civil rights. A federal Fair Employment Commission had operated during World War II with some effect, although without any statutory basis. It had died at the war's end when the House cut off its funds.

After 1950 the Truman administration had made no further major effort to pass civil rights legislation, and the incoming Eisenhower administration showed little interest in the subject. Minor maneuvering continued through the early 1950's, with dozens of bills introduced in every session to die in committee. Even though changing conditions in the South diminished the need for poll tax and lynching legislation, the old bills reappeared regularly, having acquired a symbolic and even sentimental value to their sponsors.

## Early 1956: Drafting the Bills

It was against this historical background that the Justice Department's draftsmen, in the New Year's weekend of 1956, began outlining the earliest versions of what was to become the Civil Rights Act of 1957, the first civil rights legislation to be passed by Congress since 1875.

These bills were written entirely within the Department; not only did the Department decline to ask for congressional advice, but it gave congressmen no hint of the direction in which its draftsmen were moving. (Most of the congressional experts were Democrats, and they all had their own cherished bills.) Nor did the Department consult lobbying organizations in the field, such as the National Association for the Advancement of Colored People. Brownell's first concern lay with the conservative Republicans in the Cabinet and on the White House staff. Extramural pressure groups would do him little good with the Cabinet.

Although the Civil Rights Section's initial drafts reflected a flicker of interest in the civil remedies proposed by the Truman Committee, they were primarily drawn to improve the criminal sanctions. One reason was that, within the Justice Department's structure, the Civil Rights Section was a subordinate part of the Criminal Division and had been working mainly with the criminal statutes in the past.

In the first week of January 1956, three bills were presented to Attorney General Brownell. The first was designed to broaden the Department's traditional mainstays, Sections 241 and 242 of the criminal code. The conspiracy statute, Section 241, was to be given a new clause extending it to reach individual acts not involving conspiracy. In the two *Williams* cases the Supreme Court had indicated that Section 241 was narrower than Section 242. The bill grafted some of the slightly different wording of the second statute into the first, hoping to give it equal breadth.

Convictions under Section 242 had included wanton murders, the seriousness of which had been aggravated in one case by the defendant's office as County Constable.[16] The disparity between the crime and the one-year limit on punishment called for correction. Yet the Justice Department had occasionally found it very useful to operate under a misdemeanor statute, since prosecution for a felony required an indictment but prosecution for a misdemeanor did not. (In a West Virginia case, when a grand jury had refused to indict, the Department had taken the case directly to trial by filing an information. The trial jury had convicted.[17]) As a compromise, Section 242 was to be amended to raise the penalties in violations resulting in the loss of life, but to leave them unchanged in other cases.

Most of the Department's troubles with Section 242 over the preceding decade had resulted from the *Screws* ruling that violation occurred only when a defendant knew that he was depriving his victim of a specific and defined federal right.

[16] *Crews* v. *U.S.*, 160 Fed. 2d. 746 (1947).
[17] *Catlette* v. *U.S.*, 132 Fed. 2d. 902 (1943). See Caldwell, pp. 223-224.

One solution to this requirement was an attempt to list explicitly the principal rights covered by the statute. With this in mind the draftsmen proposed a new Section, 242A, asserting fourteen rights to be protected by the bill, all of them rights previously declared by the courts. Since the subsequent congressional debates raised the question of precisely what aims the bill's authors had in mind, the tentative list of rights has a certain historical interest. It began with the right to vote and included the traditional protections against punishment without due process and against physical torture to exact testimony. It named the right to be free from segregation in attending any school or university supported by public funds. And, as a final catch-all, it asserted the right not to be deprived of any other right that had been made specific or, again a point raised in the subsequent debates, any right that might in the future be enunciated by the courts.

Another new Section, 242B, would authorize the Attorney General to bring suit in the federal district courts for injunctive enforcement of the bill's provisions. This brief paragraph was the embryo of the final version's Part III, which was to become famous on the Senate floor in 1957. Part III was fated to be cut out of the bill in 1957 when the Senate discovered that it could be used to initiate school desegregation suits, and that in years to come it could protect other rights not yet dreamed of. In its first form it said so explicitly.

While the first bill dealt with the general protection of all civil rights, the second was aimed entirely at the prevention of coercion and intimidation in voting.

The draftsmen wrote them as separate bills apparently because they overlapped and were considered, in some measure, alternatives. The Civil Rights Section was composed of professional legal specialists who were not quite sure what was going on at higher, political levels in the administration. They gave their superiors a choice. The first bill was as broad as the Section's whole experience in enforcement, but the second was much narrower and went directly to the right to a ballot.

It extended Section 594 of the criminal code, a part of the Corrupt Practices Act, to cover primary and special elections. It similarly broadened Section 1971 of Title 42, one of the Reconstruction civil statutes, which simply stated that all citizens were entitled to vote without distinction of race or color. The Civil Rights Section's draft bill declared that an individual suffering injury under Section 594 or Section 1971 could sue for redress. It then went on, in the most significant line of the bill, to grant the Attorney General authority to sue for injunctions or other relief whenever these rights were violated. In a final paragraph the bill gave the federal courts immediate jurisdiction. This provision was designed to eliminate the requirement, laid down by a federal court of appeals in a Mississippi voting case five years earlier,[18] that litigants ought to exhaust state administrative remedies before going into the federal courts.

Disfranchisement was the essential foundation upon which the whole structure of Southern racial discrimination was erected, the Civil Rights Section told Brownell. The Section argued that criminal enforcement of voting rights was so ponderous a procedure that it had little practical effect. The new provision for civil suits by the Attorney General would provide a much more effective weapon, the draftsmen suggested.

Brownell had asked for an anti-lynching bill, but the Civil Rights Section showed no great enthusiasm for it, pointing out that no lynchings had been reported in the previous four years. The draft produced was a revision of a 1948 bill, modified to avoid the most obvious constitutional difficulties in this kind of legislation. Since there was no general federally-secured right to life, language that would create in effect a federal murder statute was constitutionally questionable,

---

[18] *Peay* v. *Cox*, 190 Fed. 2d. 123 (1951). The court ruled that the plaintiff was not required to exhaust the state's judicial remedies, but Mississippi law provided a remedy that was "wholly administrative, simple, cheap and ought to be exhausted plainly."

whether or not the murderer's motive involved race and color. The Civil Rights Section suggested no more than criminal sanctions against a lynch mob, defined as a mob using violence to prevent the orderly trial and punishment of a person suspected of a crime. This much, the draftsmen felt, could be supported as a guarantee of due process. But they saw no way to extend this definition of lynching to the Till case, for example, since that had been a simple murder.

## Revisions at Higher Levels

During the month of January the Civil Rights Section's proposals underwent their first round of revisions and emerged looking less like a criminal program and more like a civil program. The Section's drafts were circulated through other offices of the Justice Department and were discussed at a series of high-level meetings within the Department. The first, on January 5, was attended by the Attorney General; his Deputy, William P. Rogers; his Executive Assistant, John V. Lindsay; the Assistant Attorney General for the Office of Legal Counsel, J. Lee Rankin; the Director of the Federal Bureau of Investigation, J. Edgar Hoover; Assistant Attorney General Olney; Arthur B. Caldwell, Chief of the Civil Rights Section; Sydney Brodie, the principal draftsman within the Civil Rights Section; and Herbert Hoffman, an assistant to the Deputy Attorney General.

The anti-lynching bill was dropped after this meeting. In addition to the objections brought up by its own authors, other lawyers within the Department questioned the fundamental constitutionality of even the careful phrases proposed by the Civil Rights Section. But the Department's high command showed a sharp interest in both of the other bills.

The pivotal meeting appears to have been held on January 26 and was attended by most of the officials who were at the earlier meeting. Their interest in civil remedies was rapidly increasing, and they renewed their search of the old, limited statutes for authority, already tested in the courts, that could be invoked to serve new and much broader purposes. It was at this point that the Department's lawyers began constructing the intricate chains of double and triple reference that were to give their final drafts an extraordinary technical complexity.

The draft that covered the full range of rights, which had begun with the two criminal statutes and ended as Part III of the consolidated bill as Congress would debate it, will hereafter be called the general civil rights bill. The draft devoted to elections, which became Part IV of the consolidated bill, will be called the voting bill.

To the general civil rights bill, the draftsmen now added amendments to the two civil statutes, Sections 1983 and 1985 of Title 42, authorizing the government to bring suits for the relief of private persons.

Another new paragraph, amending Section 1343 of Title 28, permitted these suits to be brought directly into the federal courts. That innovation was added to Section 1985 alone, on grounds that the draftsmen expected this statute to be used in voting and school cases.

In the matter of schools, the Department seemed less interested in initiating desegregation suits than in providing protection to school systems already attempting to comply with court orders. The Hoxie incident had impressed the Department with the urgent need for new law to strengthen the federal government's hand in preventing organized public resistance to the mandates of the courts.

The series of staff conferences within the Department continued through February into March. The revisions now were almost entirely aimed at cutting out the questionable or unnecessary amendments, and the effect was to reduce these two long bills to two short and terse ones. The legal technicians had had their innings in January and early February. Now political judgment dominated the drafting process. The

problem was to produce not the most effective bill conceiv-
able, but rather an effective bill likely to pass the Senate.

## The Effort to Avoid Being Inflammatory

At this stage the Department abandoned the long list of
federally-secured rights. It would have generated vehement
controversy; while each of these rights was supported by court
decisions, there was a vast difference between the assertion of a
right in one court case tied narrowly to specific facts and the
general statement of it in a statute. In any case, the list was
already under attack within the Department—on purely legal
grounds—as irremediably vague.

The draftsmen progressively weeded out changes considered nonessential. The attempt to amend Section 1983
was dropped from the general civil rights bill. The provision
for more stringent criminal sentences under Section 242 was
also given up.

At the top level the Department decided, probably early in
March, to eliminate material that might prove unnecessarily
inflammatory to the already substantial congressional opposition. In January the Civil Rights Section had been told to
prepare a list of particularly outrageous recent violations of
citizens' civil rights. That list was now permanently put aside.

The effect of this decision was clearly demonstrated in the
successive versions of the statement with which Brownell was
to present the administration program to Congress and the
public. In 1949 the Truman administration had sent its bill to
Congress with a statement running to 34 legal-size pages, plus
an appendix of five pages of statutes and another two pages on
the activities of the Civil Rights Section. It had been discursive,
full of explanation and exhortation, beginning with a recital
of the history of civil rights legislation and including the facts
of two notorious cases of murders perpetrated by Southern
peace officers. The Department at first prepared to write
something of the same sort for Brownell. But by early March

the statement had been reduced drastically, with further reductions to come. Its tone was increasingly dry and clipped. It contained no reference to any specific case; even a proposal to cite the Hoxie situation had been rejected. Its explanations of the amendments were technical and brief.

The Department seemed to be following the rule of the less said, the better. That decision was to have the greatest importance for the bill's reception in Congress, where Brownell would soon be accused of deliberately concealing the scope of the amendments.

The draftsmen had a much easier time writing the bills to establish the Civil Rights Commission and to authorize an additional Assistant Attorney General. They saw no major question of legal policy involved in either, and both followed familiar forms.

Since the President's State of the Union Message had referred specifically to a Commission, the Department wrote a bill setting up a bipartisan investigating and research panel carrying subpoena power, a weapon that Truman's 1947 Committee had not possessed. Five members were originally proposed, following a similar provision in the McGrath bill of 1949, but this was later expanded to six—to head off accusations that the Republicans intended to dominate it. This draft eventually became Part 1 of the consolidated bill.

The bill for the additional Assistant Attorney General made no reference to civil rights, according to a Departmental tradition. But the Department intended to elevate and expand the small Civil Rights Section to a full division no longer subordinate to the Criminal Division. The reorganization, which had been suggested by the Truman Committee and many other critics, was intended both to symbolize and to implement the Department's growing interest in civil remedies. Even without new legislation, the Department's increasing involvement in school cases demonstrated that the future work of its civil rights staff would reach far beyond its past preoccupation with criminal convictions, as Brownell was to point out in testimony later that year.[19] This draft was Part II of the consolidated bill.


## Pressures from Outside

While the Department was working on its bills, the pressure for civil rights legislation was building up rapidly outside the administration. On February 6 two days of rioting broke out at the University of Alabama over the admission of a Negro girl, Autherine Lucy, by order of a federal court. Once again violence illustrated the old problem of enforcing federal courts' rulings in the face of Southern defiance.

The political reaction to the riots was prompt and severe. Civil rights had appeared a few days earlier as a major issue in the competition for the Democratic nomination to the Presidency. Adlai E. Stevenson and Senator Estes Kefauver were campaigning hard for the California primary, and Kefauver had managed to give Negroes there the impression that he was taking a stronger stand for enforcement than Stevenson.[20] At a question-and-answer session with a Negro audience in Los Angeles the day after the Alabama rioting began, Stevenson was asked whether he would employ federal troops to carry out school desegregation. "It can't be done by troops or bayonets," he replied. But he went on to call integration "the most important unfulfilled promise of democracy."[21] Stevenson was promptly labeled a "moderate" on the race issue and was criticized by the more impatient of the Negro and liberal leaders.

George Meany, President of the AFL-CIO, denounced the view that "the way to handle this question is to run away from it."[22] With sharp concern, Senator Herbert H. Lehman of New

[19] U.S. Cong., Senate Committee on the Judiciary, *Hearings on Civil Rights Legislation* (Washington: U.S. GPO, 1956), p. 79.
[20] *New York Times* (hereafter *NYT*), Feb. 6, 1956.
[21] *NYT*, Feb. 12, 1956.                    [22] *NYT*, Feb. 15, 1956.

York announced that Stevenson, whom he was supporting, would soon "qualify" his position.[23]

Governor Averell Harriman of New York, an unannounced Democratic candidate for President, demanded "vigorous" federal action at the University of Alabama and declared his support of Congressman Powell's amendment to exclude segregated school districts from the pending bills for federal aid to education.[24] Stevenson opposed the Powell amendment.[25]

To complement the Autherine Lucy affair, two weeks later a Montgomery, Alabama grand jury indicted 100 leaders of the Negroes' bus boycott. It had been running since the preceding December in protest against segregated seating and alleged incivility on the part of white drivers.

At a rally in Harlem, Jacob Javits, then Republican Attorney General of New York and that year to be elected to the Senate, urged Negro Republicans to use the civil rights issue to win votes from the Democrats. He called the riots at the University of Alabama "the greatest challenge since the Civil War."[26] Vice President Richard Nixon, speaking in New York, taunted the Democrats as "helpless and futile" in dealing with the issue. He outlined progress made by the executive branch under Eisenhower and observed that the Supreme Court's school decisions were written during a Republican administration.[27]

In a characteristic contribution to the debate, Representative Powell, a Democrat representing a Harlem district, declared he would support Eisenhower against Stevenson; in his view Eisenhower had made "the greatest contribution to civil rights in the history of the United States."[28] Two weeks later in another pronouncement, he accused the President of "dodging the issue, passing the buck, trying to wash his hands like Pilate in the blood of innocent men and women in the

[23] *NYT*, Feb. 25, 1956.      [24] *NYT*, Feb. 13, 1956.
[25] *NYT*, Feb. 13, 1956.      [26] *NYT*, Feb. 11, 1956.
[27] *NYT*, Feb. 14, 1956.      [28] *NYT*, Feb. 14, 1956.

Southland." Powell added that Stevenson's position on the question was "middle-of-the-road shilly-shallying, pussyfooting, double-talking."[29]

A three-day Assembly for Civil Rights opened in Washington in early March with 2,000 delegates from a variety of labor, religious, racial, and social organizations. Clarence Mitchell, Director of the Washington Bureau of the National Association for the Advancement of Colored People, threatened that Negroes might abandon the Democratic Party on this issue.[30] Roy Wilkins, Executive Secretary of the NAACP, told the opening rally, "We have heard promise after promise. What we seek now is action, and nothing short of action— final action resulting in enactment—will suffice." The heaviest ovation of the rally was given to Miss Lucy when she appeared on the platform.

## The Congressional Bloc

In Congress there was evidence of more interest in the civil rights field than at any time since the beginning of the Eisenhower administration. Senator Thomas Hennings' Constitutional Rights Subcommittee reported a four-part proposal on March 3. It called for new legislation to protect voting rights, establishment of an additional Assistant Attorney General to handle rights cases, protection of servicemen, and federal prohibition of lynching.

For more than a year a small, informal group of representatives of both parties had been meeting to discuss civil rights strategy. The leader among the Republicans was Hugh Scott of Philadelphia. Other Republicans were John W. Heselton of Deerfield, Massachusetts and Charles A. Wolverton of Camden, New Jersey. Among the Democrats were two

[29] *NYT*, March 3, 1956; *Washington Post* (hereafter *Post*), March 3, 1956.
[30] *NYT*, March 5, 1956.

of the three Negro congressmen, Powell and Charles C. Diggs, Jr. of Detroit. There was James Roosevelt of Los Angeles and, on occasion, Emanuel Celler of Brooklyn, New York. And there was a soft-spoken and influential young Missourian, Richard Bolling of Kansas City, in his fourth term and a member of the Rules Committee.

Scott and his colleagues decided, probably late in 1955 and certainly by mid-January of 1956,[31] to concentrate their efforts on voting legislation. Apparently they came to this decision independently of the Justice Department's specialists. Through Scott this small bloc had been pressing the Department for assistance from the administration, and the first public word of the new bills came from Scott. He told a reporter on January 12 that the administration was drafting a message to contain "specific proposals for legislation."[32]

Brownell and Scott, the most active Republican campaigners for civil rights legislation in the Cabinet and in the House, had remarkably similar backgrounds. Both had entered politics in large Eastern cities with substantial Negro populations. Brownell had represented a Manhattan constituency for five terms in the New York State Legislature. Scott's district was five wards of Philadelphia. Brownell had been Chairman of the Republican National Committee during the first Dewey campaign, Scott during the second. Both had worked closely with General Eisenhower in the organization of the 1952 campaign. In their work in the presidential campaigns, these experienced legislators had acquired the national and presidential view of American politics, as opposed to the local and congressional view.

The Democrats within this congressional bloc were ham-

---

[31] Drew Pearson, in a column reporting a meeting in Scott's office, said the group decided to abandon fair employment legislation and turn to voting and physical protection, i.e., an anti-lynching bill: *Post*, Jan. 12, 1956. According to another account given the author, the decision to concentrate on voting was taken the preceding December, and lynching was not under consideration.

[32] *NYT*, Jan. 13, 1956.

pered by competition among themselves. On a smaller scale, this group began to show symptoms of the same inability to agree on leadership that the liberal Democrats in the Senate were to demonstrate the following year. Scott, who handled administration liaison, was also a member of both the Rules and the Judiciary Committees; in the bloc's occasional public pronouncements during these months he was the Republicans' spokesman. But each time he had a different Democratic counterpart.

In November Powell announced the group's "formation," although it had been meeting for a year or so. As its "co-ordinator," Powell added, he intended to appoint a member of his own staff. He identified the leadership as himself, Scott, Diggs, and Mitchell of the NAACP.[33] Another meeting of the bloc was called in mid-February by Scott and Diggs. The bloc was expanded in late February; 26 congressmen of both parties attended a meeting called to explore means of expediting legislation. An executive committee of six was set up under Scott and, this time, Edna F. Kelly, Democrat of Brooklyn. It was to contact the Judiciary Committee and the Justice Department and report back in two weeks.[34] It never did so publicly, for in early March it became known that the Department was about to present a program going well beyond the President's proposed Commission.

In late February columnist Drew Pearson reported that the Department was about to enter bills asserting federal rights in state and local elections.[35] The first Washington newspaper to obtain more precise information was the Scripps-Howard tabloid, the *Daily News*, which announced a week later that the administration was pondering a plan to give the Attorney General a stronger hand in the enforcement of Negroes' voting rights. This account, while not complete, was as good

[33] *Post*, Nov. 18, 1955.
[34] *Washington Evening Star*, Feb. 22, 1956.
[35] *Post*, Feb. 12, 1956.

as any that appeared in the next month. The writer cited three proposals: the Commission, the new Assistant Attorney General, and "extension and definition of the avenues of civil action—the right to obtain injunctions and assess civil penalties—to supplement existing criminal statutes applicable to this field."[36] The *New York Times* said, two days later, that the Department was preparing "legislation that would give it the right to intervene in alleged rights violations on its own initiative and which would specifically outlaw any economic or physical threats against exercise of the right to vote."[37]

In this fashion the tag, "a voting bill," was firmly affixed to the Department's program well before it appeared in public. This tag endured through more than a year of congressional scrutiny, in spite of a continuous Southern outcry, largely discounted, and the Attorney General's testimony in early 1957 before both Senate and House committees that it would have applied to schools, at least in the Hoxie case.[38] The label endured partly because the bill applied explicitly to voting but only implicitly to schools, and partly because Congress was anticipating a voting bill. Some of Scott's group, for instance, thought it was based on their ideas. When the bill finally arrived, its congressional supporters saw mainly what they expected to see.

But by the first week of March 1956 it was clear that the Department's proposals were going to involve far more than the mild, vague suggestions in the State of the Union Message. It was clear, too, that Brownell was preparing to carry these proposals to Congress soon. New Jersey's two Republican senators, H. Alexander Smith and Clifford Case, discussed the

---

[36] *Washington Daily News*, March 5, 1956.
[37] *NYT*, March 7.
[38] U.S. Cong., House, Subcommittee No. 5 of the Committee on the Judiciary, *Hearings on Civil Rights*, 85th Cong., 1st Sess., 1957, p. 605. Senate, Subcommittee on Constitutional Rights, *Hearings, Civil Rights*, 85th Cong., 1st Sess., 1957, pp. 7-8.

matter with Brownell on March 7 and were permitted to announce that the program would reach the Capitol within a few days.[39]

## The White House Refuses to Clear Brownell's Program

Suddenly Brownell ran into trouble from an unexpected source. The White House refused to clear the program. Apparently the Republican leader in the Senate, William F. Knowland of California, ignited this opposition. According to one account, Knowland read the *New York Times*' description of the program and protested, immediately and effectively, to the White House.

Two days after Brownell delivered his optimistic prediction to the New Jersey senators, he took the four bills and his accompanying statement to the Cabinet. Here he collided with the President's personal opinions, which were supported by most of his Cabinet. The bills had been written at a time, after the President's heart attack, when the President's retirement from office had seemed probable.[40] But he had recuperated strongly and on February 29 had announced that he would run for re-election. By this time it was too late for any profound revisions of the bills even if the Department had wished to undertake them. Instead of receiving from the President and the Cabinet a free hand to proceed, Brownell now found himself confronted by the President's own firm, and frequently reiterated, policy.

The Department was taking the position that if the Constitution guaranteed rights to the citizen, it was the government's duty to try to secure those rights. The President, however, was instinctively opposed to coercion in what seemed to him a matter, not of simple law enforcement, but of allowing the South to catch up with a changing law. His Solicitor Gen-

[39] *NYT*, March 8.
[40] For example, *NYT*, columns by James Reston, Jan. 20, 26, 1956.

eral had argued the school cases, but the President had never personally taken a position on the rights and wrongs of school desegregation.[41]

## The President's Position on Civil Rights

Eisenhower was later accused of inconstancy in his views on civil rights. But his views were consistent with his conception of the Presidency as the great reconciling force in national affairs, and himself as a mediator and defender of law and order rather than a partisan in domestic politics. Regarding racial relations in the South, President Eisenhower spelled out this attitude with great clarity in a series of press conferences in the first three months of 1956.

He spoke with sympathy of the Southerners' deep attachment to their traditions, but he reiterated that they must necessarily, in the end, lose their great struggle.

"Let us remember," he said on March 14, "that the Supreme Court itself talked about emotionalism in this question, and it was for that reason that it said, 'progress must be gradual.' " The President continued:

> Now, let us not forget there has been some progress. I believe there is something on the order of more than a quarter of a million of Negro children in the border and some Southern states that have been integrated in the schools, and except for a certain area in which the difficulties are greatest, there has been progress. . . .
> So, let us remember that there are people who are ready to approach this thing with moderation, but with determination to make progress that the Supreme Court asked for. If there

[41] Nor would he do so when the challenge to federal authority became direct and explicit; see Corinne Silverman, *The Little Rock Story* (ICP No. 41), University of Alabama Press, 1959. Eisenhower did not personally endorse the school decision as legally and morally correct until a press interview on October 8, 1963, when he was in retirement.

ever was a time when we must be patient without being complacent, when we must be understanding of other people's deep emotions as well as our own, this is it. Extremists on neither side are going to help this situation, and we can only believe that the good sense, the common sense of Americans will bring this thing along. The length of time I am not even going to talk about; I don't know anything about the length of time it will take.[42]

The President refused to take sides in the increasingly rancorous in-fighting in Congress. Reporters asked him four times that winter about the Powell amendment, which had thrown the school construction bill into the controversial segregation issue.

"This is what I believe," the President replied the first time. "The school construction bill should be passed. Now if Congress wants to put the other [the Powell amendment] on, and does it, I will understand why they are doing it. But I just simply say, let's get the school bill; that is what I want."[43] He brushed off later inquiries brusquely. In March he said, "I am not going to make any declaration in advance of any law that is placed in front of me. I never do, and I want to see the law first."[44] The 1956 school bill was subsequently drowned in the quicksand of racial controversy.

Eisenhower regarded federal intervention as the last resort in meeting even the most violent disorders. He was asked, immediately after the Autherine Lucy riots, whether he would order the Justice Department to investigate. He replied that the Department always looked into possible violations of federal law.

"But you must remember," he continued, "the Supreme Court decision turned this whole process of integration back to the district courts, and the district courts were specifically instructed to handle it under the conditions that apply locally, so far as they can."

[42] *Presidential Papers*, p. 304.        [43] *Ibid.*, p. 187.
[44] *Ibid.*, p. 303.

While there has been an outbreak that all of us deplore, when there is a defiance of law, still the chancellor and trustees [of the University of Alabama], the local authorities, the student body and all the rest of them have not yet had an opportunity, I should think, to settle this thing as it ought to be settled. I would certainly hope that we could avoid any interference with anybody else as long as that state, from its Governor on down, will do its best to straighten it out.[45]

Even the most blunt expressions of Southern defiance Eisenhower turned away with soft answers, refusing to read them as either threats to the government or challenges to himself. The Southerners' most extreme pronouncements attacked the desegregation decisions and the Court. Eisenhower considered himself a bystander in this dispute.

William V. Shannon of the *New York Post* asked him, at a news conference on February 29, to comment on the interposition resolutions passed by four Southern states, and the federal role in enforcing integration. The President replied:

Well, of course, you have asked a very vast question that is filled with argument on both sides. You have raised the question of States' Rights and Federal power; you have particularly brought up the question whether the Supreme Court is the last word we have in the interpretation of our Constitution.

Now, this is what I say: There are adequate legal means of determining all of these factors. The Supreme Court has issued its own operational directives and delegated power to the district courts.

I expect that we are going to make progress, and the Supreme Court itself said it does not expect revolutionary action suddenly executed. We will make progress, and I am not going to attempt to tell them how it is going to be done.[46]

The same question was put even more forcefully two weeks later, after the Southern Manifesto had been presented to Congress. Signed by 100 Southern senators and representa-

[45] *Ibid.*, pp. 233-234.        [46] *Ibid.*, pp. 269-270.

tives, it was read to the Senate by Walter F. George of Georgia and was introduced in the House by Howard W. Smith of Virginia on March 12, 1956.

"The unwarranted decision of the Supreme Court in the public school cases is now bearing the fruit always produced when men substitute naked power for established law," the Manifesto began. "We regard the decision of the Supreme Court in the school cases as a clear abuse of judicial power. . . . This unwarranted exercise of power by the Court, contrary to the Constitution, is creating chaos and confusion in the States primarily affected. . . . Without regard to the consent of the governed, outside agitators are threatening immediate and revolutionary changes in our public school systems."

The signers declared their reliance upon the Constitution as the "fundamental law of the land," but decried the Court's "encroachments" upon the constitutional rights of their states and their people.

"We commend the motives of those States which have declared the intention to resist forced integration by any lawful means. . . . We pledge ourselves to use all lawful means to bring about a reversal of this decision which is contrary to the Constitution and to prevent the use of force in its implementation," the Manifesto continued. It ended with an appeal to the Southern people "not to be provoked by agitators and troublemakers" into disorder and lawlessness.[47]

The question of defiance was put to Eisenhower at his March 14 press conference. Edward P. Morgan of the American Broadcasting Company suggested that the Manifesto was a "direct challenge" by the South, and that it carried an "implied" threat to block the confirmation of judges.

"Well, you are asking a question that we are probably going to be busy on for a while," the President mildly observed.

First, I have nothing whatsoever to say about their right to confirm or not confirm. The constitutional duty of the

[47] *Congressional Record*, 84th Cong., 2d Sess., 1956, p. 4460.

Senate to act as it sees fit upon the nominations sent up by the President is clear. I could urge publicly, and I probably would if I thought there were unnecessary blocks, but that is their business and that doesn't call, as I see it, for any further comment. Now, the first thing about the Manifesto is this: that they say they are going to use every legal means. No one in any responsible position anywhere has talked nullification; there would be a place where we get to a very bad spot for the simple reason I am sworn to defend and uphold the Constitution of the United States and of course I can never abandon or refuse to carry out my own duty.[48]

Morgan brought the Manifesto up again at the next news conference, asking whether Eisenhower would accept the support in the fall election of Southern Democrats who had expressed their "defiance" of the court. Eisenhower answered:

I don't believe they have expressed their defiance. I believe they expressed the belief that it was in error, and they have talked about using legal means to circumvent or to get it, whatever the expression they have used.

I do not believe that anyone, the ones that I know, have used the words "defy the Supreme Court," because when we carry this to the ultimate, remember that the Constitution, as interpreted by the Supreme Court, is our basic law.[49]

Repeatedly Eisenhower sounded the theme that "the basic law appears to change."

Now let us remember this one thing, and it is very important: the people who have this deep emotional reaction on the other side were not acting over these past three generations in defiance of law. They were acting in compliance with the law as interpreted by the Supreme Court of the United States under the decision of 1896. Now, that has been completely reversed, and it is going to take time for them to adjust their thinking and their progress to that.[50]

[48] *Presidential Papers*, pp. 303-304.
[49] *Ibid.*, p. 340. See also Robert J. Donovan, *Eisenhower, the Inside Story* (New York: Harper and Brothers, 1956), p. 391.
[50] *Presidential Papers*, p. 305. The case referred to is *Plessy* v. *Ferguson*, 163 U.S. 537.

We are not talking here about coercing, using force in a general way; we are simply going to uphold the Constitution of the United States, see that the program made as ordered by them is carried out. . . . I have never yet given up my belief that the American people, faced with a great problem like this, will approach it intelligently and with understanding, and we will get somewhere. . . .[51]

The President's policy was the hopeful one that a soft answer turneth away wrath. By the winter's end, between the Autherine Lucy case and the Democratic primaries, the weight of the evidence was running increasingly to the contrary.

## The Cabinet Meeting, March 9, 1956

On March 9 Brownell submitted to the Cabinet the four bills and the formal explanatory statement that was to accompany the bills to Congress. In it he summarized the arguments for relying on civil sanctions rather than criminal, and for removing the civil rights staff from the Criminal Division of his Department. Accompanying Brownell to the Cabinet meeting, presumably to bolster the case for new legislation, was the Director of the Federal Bureau of Investigation, J. Edgar Hoover. However, Hoover's half-hour talk only reinforced the President's inclination toward passivity.

Hoover began by observing that racial tension had been rising steadily since the school decisions appeared. He had noted an increasing tendency toward violent language among segregationists. Reviewing the proponent organizations, Hoover reported that the Communist Party showed great interest in this issue and had made attempts to infiltrate the NAACP, which had nonetheless reaffirmed its anti-Communist position. To give an example of Communist propaganda activity, Hoover said that in September 1955 the Party began agitation over the Till murder, calling upon the President to fire the Attorney General. On September 2, he continued, Mayor Richard J. Daley of Chicago had wired the President urging

[51] *Ibid.*, p. 305.

his intervention in the case. Daley was not a Communist, Hoover said, but the incident seemed to him to demonstrate the potency of the pressures instigated by the Communists. There was also evidence, he added, that a Communist leader had conferred with NAACP officials about the recent Civil Rights Assembly held in Washington, and the Communists had planned to use the Assembly to divide the administration and the Southern Democrats who supported it. The Party hoped in this fashion to influence the 1956 elections, Hoover stated. He observed that the Communist program demanded federal intervention, with troops if necessary, to enforce order and protect civil rights in the Deep South.

Among the other proponents of civil rights legislation Hoover listed the Afro-American Congress of Christian Organizations and the Muslim Cult of Islam, two racist Negro groups.

The FBI Director then turned to the proliferation of segregationist organizations in the preceding three years and the efforts to revive the Ku Klux Klan. He described some of the economic sanctions being used to enforce discrimination. But violence, particularly lynchings, had dropped off in recent years, he asserted, and the attitude of Southern law enforcement authorities toward civil rights cases was improving.

"Calm, judicious judgment, public education, and real understanding are needed to avert explosive incidents," Hoover concluded. "The area of danger lies in friction between extremists on both sides ready with violence."[52]

The Cabinet was unenthusiastic about Brownell's program. "Stassen did not think any of Brownell's recommendations had a chance of being passed by Congress," the President's Chief Assistant, Sherman Adams, later wrote.[53] "Benson suggested waiting a few years until the Republicans gained control of the Senate and the House. The Georgia-born Marion Folsom,

[52] A heavily edited version of this report is contained in Donovan, pp. 389-391.
[53] Sherman Adams, *First Hand Report* (New York: Popular Library, 1962), p. 332.

whose Health, Education, and Welfare Department's pro-
grams would be affected by the racial issue, felt that, in
asking for anything more than the Civil Rights Commission,
Brownell was pointing to the conclusions that he wanted the
commission to reach. I said that the whole package would be
accepted by Congress only if careful planning were given to
the timing and the manner of approach used in its presentation,
and the President then asked Brownell to bring the program
back to the Cabinet again for more discussion before he sent
it to the Hill."

The following week, since there was no Cabinet meeting,
Brownell circulated his revision among the Cabinet members. The only change was a new preamble to his explanatory
statement, picking up some of the tone of the presidential press
conferences. A new paragraph declared that interpretation
of existing law was the courts' job, but the law as the courts
defined it must be obeyed. It went on to emphasize the necessity of restraint and compassion in a matter of profound
emotional importance. But the bills were not changed in
substance.

In the middle of March, Special Counsel to the President
Gerald D. Morgan conferred with Justice Department officials. Morgan was the top man in the executive branch's
legislative clearance machinery. He recommended limiting the
voting bill to civil enforcement; accordingly, the amendment
of Section 594, Title 18, was dropped. At this conference the
amendment of Title 28, giving federal courts direct jurisdiction, was cut out of the civil rights bill. In the last round of
minor adjustments over the next two weeks, however, the
Title 28 amendment was dropped from the voting bill but
was restored to the general civil rights bill.

## Cabinet Meeting, March 23

The four bills and the Brownell statement went back to the
Cabinet on March 23. The statement was amended a little

further, bringing in still more of the spirit of the President's news conferences. It now declared that only a reliance upon law could prevent extremists from causing great damage. This, in turn, made the flexibility of civil remedies particularly desirable, it argued. The four bills were now in the form in which they would finally go to Congress.

At this Cabinet meeting the division was precisely the same as two weeks earlier. As Sherman Adams later recalled:

> Wilson said that the racial issue was hot enough without adding more fuel to it. . . . Dulles said he was strongly convinced that laws which departed from the established customs of the people were impractical. Eisenhower mentioned that after a recent talk with Billy Graham he had come to the conclusion that, as a result of recent tensions, some of the hard-won advances in recent years toward better race relations had actually been lost. . . . But Arthur Flemming and Mitchell backed Brownell in contending that the statement in the President's State of the Union message had promised a strong civil rights program and that a proposal for a Civil Rights Commission would be inadequate. Faced by this rift of opinion in the Cabinet, Eisenhower asked the Attorney General to hold up the program until they had discussed it together.[54]

That meeting was on a Friday; on the following Monday Republican congressional leaders were told that the program would arrive that Wednesday. The *New York Times* caught wind of it, and reported on Tuesday that it would be announced the following day.[55]

Once again it hung fire. The United Press reported on Wednesday that the bills would not appear until after the congressional Easter recess, which was to end on April 9.[56] The newspapers were still under the impression that the program included no more than the Commission, the addi-

[54] *Ibid.*, p. 333.  [55] *NYT*, March 28.
[56] *Post*, March 29, 1956.

tional Assistant Attorney General, and some sort of civil redress in voting cases.[57]

When they heard of these further unexplained delays, some
members of the civil rights bloc in the House threatened to
bring a bill of their own to the floor. Subcommittee Number
Two of the House Judiciary Committee had held hearings the
previous July on 51 civil rights bills. It was now prepared to
report two of them, one an anti-lynching statute and the
other, H.R. 627, an omnibus bill introduced by the Chairman
of the full Committee, Emanuel Celler. But in voting to clear
the bills, the ranking minority member of the Subcommittee,
William E. Miller of Buffalo, New York, had obtained a
promise from the Chairman, Thomas J. Lane of Lawrence,
Massachusetts that the full Committee would take no action
until Brownell had an opportunity to "submit his views."[58]

Heselton, a Republican, pointed out on Wednesday, March
28, that two Democrats, Roosevelt and Charles B. Brownson
of Indiana, had already introduced resolutions for the consideration of H.R. 627. If neither the administration nor the
Committee acted, Heselton warned, a discharge petition
would be introduced immediately after the recess.

On April 2, Celler announced that he had invited Brownell
to testify on April 10. Kenneth B. Keating of Rochester, New
York, ranking minority member of the Judiciary Committee,
announced on April 4 that the administration program would
appear the following week, and he intended to sponsor it.
But there appeared to be doubt as to whether Brownell himself would appear before the Committee, and whether he
would be ready to propose specific legislation. The *New York
Times* reported on April 6, "It was said today he might send a
spokesman. . . . It was indicated that the Administration's
program had not taken final form."[59]

[57] See the newspaper articles to which the two preceding notes refer;
also, a column by James Reston, *NYT*, Apr. 3.
[58] U.S. Cong., House Committee on the Judiciary, *Hearing on Civil
Rights Legislation*, 84th Cong., 2d. Sess., Apr. 10, 1956, pp. 9-10.
[59] *NYT*, Apr. 6, 1956.

## The White House Orders Two Bills Dropped

Suddenly, during the first week of April, the long, tense negotiations between the White House and the Justice Department were ended with a decision that staggered the Department. The White House denied clearance to the general civil rights and voting bills. It meant dropping all of the new enforcement authority from the program, stripping it merely to a bill setting up the Commission and a bill authorizing a new Assistant Attorney General.

The Department hastily rewrote Brownell's statement. But, significantly, the changes were the fewest possible. In the paragraphs covering enforcement, the references to accompanying bills were deleted. Instead, Brownell urged Congress and the proposed Commission to consider the recommended "changes." But the argument for civil enforcement procedures and the outlines of the specific amendments to achieve them were left intact. The statement, in the form of letters to the Vice President and the Speaker of the House,[60] was made public April 9, the day Congress reconvened. Attached to these letters were the texts of the two surviving bills.

Congressional reaction was mixed. Senator Hubert H. Humphrey, Democrat of Minnesota, called the program "lip service by leap-year liberals." Senator Richard B. Russell, Democrat of Georgia, assailed it as "cheap politics." Senator Case said he would sponsor bills to enact the program but added a hope that the President would call a conference "to discuss the immediate problems of public school integration."[61]

The press generally seized Brownell's statement as a whole, and made no distinction between those parts of it for which bills were submitted, and those for which he merely asked "consideration."[62]

[60] The letter to the Vice President appears in Senate Committee on the Judiciary, *Hearings on Civil Rights Legislation*, 85th Cong., 1st Sess., 1957, pp. 65-67. The two letters were identical.
[61] *NYT*, Apr. 10, 1956.
[62] For example, *NYT*, Apr. 10, 1956.

When the House Judiciary Committee convened the next morning, Brownell was there. It was an executive session, and newspaper reporters were not admitted. Brownell described the "four matters" mentioned in the letter to the Speaker,[63] making no distinction between the two bills and the two suggestions. When he finished, Celler began to question him.

## Brownell Gets the Other Two Bills Introduced

Keating broke in. The Justice Department had privately warned him beforehand of the White House's refusal to clear the enforcement bills. Keating, by prearrangement, made this request:

> In your communications, Mr. Attorney General, to the Speaker of the House and the Vice President enclosing two specific bills, you made these other recommendations and urged a consideration by the Congress and the proposed bipartisan commission of three specific changes. I wanted to ask you whether you had in legislative form or could get in legislative form the specific recommendations which you made in your letter as an aid to this committee. In general I am in accord with your recommendations, and I would like to put them into legislative form if we could have your assistance in that regard.[64]

"We could do that very easily, Mr. Congressman, and we would be very happy to do that," Brownell replied.

Francis E. Walter, Democrat of Easton, Pennsylvania observed that the proposed commission was to spend two years studying the need for legislation. "Do I understand you to mean that we should not legislate until this commission has completed its study?" Walter asked.

"Let me put it this way, Congressman," Brownell explained.

> We think there should be immediate action on the bills to create the commission and to set up the new assistant attorney general. I don't see how anybody really, all things

[63] U.S. Cong., House Committee on the Judiciary, 84th Cong., 2d Sess., 1956, p. 11.
[64] The following conversation is reported in *Ibid.*, pp. 19-20.

considered, would want to oppose those at the present time.

Now, as to these other proposals that we make, I personally feel that they should be passed now. We have said in our communication to the Speaker that this is for the consideration of the Congress and of the bipartisan commission. We naturally leave it up to you as to how to do that. I think that the need for them has been sufficiently demonstrated, so that I would be happy to see the Congress pass all of these proposals at the present time.

Brownell had no license from the White House to go so far.

Celler, who had not spent 32 years listening to administration witnesses for nothing, pounced on the key word.

"You said, 'personally,' " he pointed out.

"Yes," said Brownell.

"You speak for the Administration, do you not?" Celler asked.

With the question put bluntly, Brownell could return only one answer.

Yes. I think I am authorized to say, as the letter in fact points out, that these are submitted for the consideration of Congress. I also say that if the Congress doesn't pass them at this session, important as we think they are, then we certainly want them considered by the Commission.

After the hearing, a reporter asked Brownell why the administration program had arrived so late in the year. The Attorney General blandly replied that the Commission had been proposed by the President in January, and that the request for an additional Assistant Attorney General had been before Congress for the past fifteen years.[65]

The two enforcement bills were shot up to the Capitol that afternoon by special messenger. Keating, Scott, and Miller introduced them the next day.[66] In the bureaucracy's term for it, the bills were being "bootlegged up to the Hill."

[65] *Post*, Apr. 11, 1956.
[66] The commission and Assistant Attorney General bills were introduced Apr. 9 by Keating (H.R. 10340 and H.R. 10339) and by Scott (H.R. 10349 and H.R. 10348) and on Apr. 10 by Miller (H.R. 10378

Brownell received less immediate co-operation in the Senate. Senator Everett M. Dirksen of Illinois, the Republican whip, and seventeen other senators promptly introduced the two bills attached to the letter to the Vice President.[67] But it was not until April 24 that the two enforcement measures were introduced, this time by Senator Case of New Jersey. Dirksen was among the thirteen co-sponsors.[68]

In the Senate Judiciary Committee, Brownell faced a particularly difficult situation. The Chairman, James O. Eastland of Mississippi, had no intention of allowing action on any civil rights legislation at all. And the Chairman of the Constitutional Rights Subcommittee, Hennings, a dedicated supporter of civil rights legislation, deeply resented the Attorney General's refusal over the years to comment upon the legislation being developed by the Subcommittee. Furthermore, by this time Hennings was already committed to a somewhat different program of his own.

Brownell appeared before the Senate Judiciary Committee on May 16. Taking up the four bills one by one, he noted that the first two had accompanied the letter to the Vice President. Of the third he said only, "We have put these provisions in a third bill," and of the last, "A bill embodying these proposals was drafted in the Department."[69] Hennings and Brownell then argued over the Justice Department's failure to answer Hennings' letters concerning his Subcommittee's bills.

In the weeks after the bills went to Congress, the White House maintained a glacial silence on the subject. Finally, on April 17, at a meeting of Republican legislative leaders, Eisenhower observed "that he had gone over these proposals

---

and H.R. 10379). The general civil rights bill and the voting bill were introduced on Apr. 11 by Keating as H.R. 10427 and H.R. 10425, by Scott as H.R. 10428 and H.R. 10426, and by Miller as 10435 and 10434.

[67] S. 3605 and S. 3604, both introduced Apr. 11.

[68] S. 3717 and S. 3718.

[69] U.S. Cong., Senate Committee on the Judiciary, *Hearings on Civil Rights Legislation*, 84th Cong., 2d. Sess., 1956, pp. 81, 84.

very carefully and he did not see how they could be more moderate or less provocative."[70] He lectured the leaders on the virtue of moderation. The White House staff members understood Brownell's maneuver, but they were hardly in a position to tell the public, in an election year, that the administration's civil rights bills were not supported by the administration.

In his astonishingly bold tactics, Brownell had deliberately jeopardized his own office to get this set of powerful bills introduced; it appeared that he had, as a Cabinet member, overstepped the line that divided initiative from insubordination. The lengths to which he had gone to bring out the bills nearly caused their death at a later stage. To get the bills through the White House, or more accurately around it, he had been forced to conceal their import; and none but a few specialists quite understood them until a moment of appalled enlightenment was to burst on the congressional debate fifteen months later. In that moment the country was to be much surprised at the President's refusal to defend legislation that bore his imprimatur.

[70] *Adams*, p. 334.

# ( II )

# Congress
# Deals with the 1956 Bill

In Congress, the administration's 1956 civil rights program got off to a dubious start. The calendar alone left very little hope for its passage. April was late for the introduction of any major legislation, and in a presidential election year, the conventions usually set an inflexible terminus to the session and made an extremely effective weapon of simple delay.

Brownell's reputation for disingenuous maneuver compounded the administration's difficulties. The early history of the civil rights bill never became public. It appeared that Eisenhower's personal support for a new civil rights law was at best tepid. Many congressmen guessed that Brownell had gone considerably farther than the President wished. Some immediately concluded that Brownell had prepared the bills only to embarrass the Democrats, and had timed their arrival deliberately to produce a maximum of discord among the opposition without risking passage and jeopardizing Eisenhower's substantial strength in the South.

The NAACP was under the impression that the bills had been finished at the beginning of the year and had been purposefully sat on until it was too late to hope for enactment. The *Washington Post* introduced the civil rights program to its readers as one "likely to produce far more political agitation than legislation. . . ." "It is not surprising," the *Richmond Times-Dispatch* sourly commented in an editorial on April 12, "that numerous politicians from the North and West, including President Eisenhower and Attorney General Brownell, should be whooping it up for 'civil rights' in this election year. Such gestures have come to be almost as inevitable as the party conventions."

The bills put the Democratic leadership in an uncomfortable tactical position. The *New York Times* observed in an arch editorial on April 27: "We would not go so far as to say that Attorney General Brownell pushed for this particular measure at this particular time just to accomplish this particular purpose; but the sudden flurry of interest so late in the Congressional session is enough to make one wonder." A month later another *Times* editorial added: "The most interesting thing about this series of proposals is that the Administration did not see fit to embody them in legislative form sooner than the spring of this Presidential election year, when they would be calculated to cause maximum embarassment to the Democratic party."

Such assessments of Brownell's intention persisted throughout the session. Even at its end, columnist Joseph Alsop wrote:

> . . . if the Eisenhower Administration had had the faintest serious desire to pass a civil rights bill, the bill would have been introduced at the beginning of the session and pushed with maximum power thereafter. Instead, the Administration bill was only offered in May [sic], when it had no possible chance of getting past the usual roadblock of a Southern filibuster. The sole intention, obviously, was to encourage the Democrats to stage an intraparty Donnybrook Fair. The trick savored of that peculiar brand of slick political smartness for which Attorney General Herbert Brownell is widely and justly celebrated.[1]

[1] *Post*, July 29.

From the beginning, the administration did nothing to counter the general assumption that the civil rights bill would expire in the Senate. Even its spokesmen in Congress were restrained. The best that Representative Keating could offer on April 9 was an estimate that the proposals "have an excellent chance at least on the House side." Asked for a prognosis, Senator Knowland said the Commission and the additional Assistant Attorney General might be established, but this was "as far as you can go this session."[2]

Although enactment seemed hopeless, many civil rights advocates wanted the bill to pass the House at least. Legislators in both parties believed House passage would dramatize the issue and create a momentum that might carry over into the succeeding administration. Many House members from the Northern industrial cities wanted a chance to vote on a civil rights bill before the election. The liberals intended to force a fight, and neither party's leadership could risk open opposition. The Republicans had to recognize that it was, after all, part of the President's legislative program. The Democrats were acutely aware of the importance of civil rights in the presidential primaries; for Stevenson to be nominated as a "moderate" on civil rights after the Democratic majority in Congress had let the administration bill die would have been a poor beginning to an autumn campaign already likely to be difficult.

Only one man could have stopped the bill under these circumstances: Speaker Sam Rayburn of Bonham, Texas. By things left unsaid and undone, rather than by any affirmative commitment, the Speaker had given his Party's liberals a clear impression that he would not block the bill if it could be brought to the floor.

The House had passed a civil rights bill eight times since 1937, twice in the 81st Congress.[3] Most significant had been Adam Clayton Powell's 1950 bill for a Fair Employment Practices Commission, which the South had fought as bitterly

[2] *Post*, Apr. 10.
[3] Legislative Reference Service list prepared for Senator Knowland.

as any bill ever introduced. But all previous civil rights bills either had been prevented from reaching the Senate floor or had been successfully filibustered there.

The South's chief strategist in 1956 was the Chairman of the Rules Committee, Howard Worth Smith of Broad Run, Virginia. An experienced tactician and a realist, Smith knew that the bill would be passed if it came to a vote on the floor. Smith also realized that it would be very difficult, and probably impossible, to prevent it from coming to a vote eventually. The critical question, then, would be the date of passage. If it were to come at the end of the session, none of the Senate's leaders would be likely to invite chaos by attempting to call up the bill. Obstruction by a minority of the House could not stave off civil rights legislation forever, but if it were carried out competently, it could prevent action in 1956. The best tactic for the South seemed simple delay.

The preliminary skirmish in 1956 introduced practically all of the issues around which the debates of 1957 would revolve. It revealed the pitfalls that the following year's highly sophisticated strategies were designed to avoid. The parliamentary traps that were set and sprung in 1956 explain much of the 1957 maneuver.

## The Primaries Intensify the Issue

As Congress waited for the civil rights battle to open, the issue developed rapidly throughout the country. The question of racial relations had become extremely important in the acerbic competition between Stevenson and Kefauver for the Democratic presidential nomination. The pressure on the Democratic leadership in Congress rose and fell with the pattern of the primary returns.

Four states' primaries overshadowed all the others.[4] The

[4] C. A. H. Thomson and Frances M. Shattuck, *The 1956 Presidential Campaign* (Washington: The Brookings Institution, 1960).

first was Minnesota's, on March 20, and Stevenson went into it with the unanimous backing of the ranking Party leaders there. The result was very nearly a catastrophe for him. Kefauver campaigned hard and effectively, using the charge of "bossism" to turn Stevenson's impressive party support into a weapon against him. Kefauver won twenty-six delegates to Stevenson's four.

The probable nominee, Stevenson, campaigned with the autumn general election constantly in mind. He wanted the support of a united Democratic Party. As the underdog, Kefauver played on the Party's inner divisions where they offered advantages for the convention. Kefauver was creating "hostilities and divisions" among the Democrats, Stevenson charged angrily in early April.[5]

Whenever the candidates went into the South, they were immediately challenged on the race issue. Before a round of speeches in Florida in April, Stevenson took a brief vacation at the Guggenheim plantation near Kingsland, Georgia and was interviewed by M. L. St. John, political editor of the *Atlanta Constitution*, his most powerful advocate among the Southern newspapers. Explaining the difficulty of the middle position, Stevenson went on to say:

> But it also becomes more and more important that the mediator's role be filled. The hope that I could fill that role, in both the domestic and foreign fields, is the only satisfaction I get out of seeking the Presidency again. The fate of the world depends on unity among Americans. . . . To have that unity we must settle the segregation problem peaceably, honorably, and according to our law, our conscience and our religion.[6]

The following day Stevenson told St. John that "it would be unmitigated disaster if the South should leave the Democratic party because of a civil rights dispute."[7]

[5] *NYT*, Apr. 3, 1956.          [6] *Atlanta Constitution*, Apr. 5.
[7] *Constitution*, Apr. 6.

Senator Allen Ellender of Louisiana predicted a Southern bolt if either Kefauver or Governor Harriman of New York were nominated. But Stevenson had "considerably tempered" his views since 1952, the Senator said, and was acceptable.[8] A month later Herman Talmadge, former Governor of Georgia and a candidate for the Senate, said he preferred Stevenson and declined to comment on the possibility of a third party.[9] In reply Kefauver drew cheers from an audience of University of California students with a declaration that he did not take his civil rights position from Talmadge.[10]

After their defeat in Minnesota, Stevenson's managers cast hastily about for an opportunity to recoup lost prestige. They chose to enter the Oregon primary on May 18; the filing deadline was long past, but both Stevenson and Kefauver organized vigorous write-in campaigns. This time Stevenson won, with about sixty percent of the vote.

The third major primary was in Florida, on May 29, and here the race issue was paramount. Stevenson had the upper hand in organizational strength; six of the seven Democratic congressmen endorsed him. Both candidates declared the Supreme Court's desegregation decisions were the law and must be obeyed. But one of the curiosities of color politics seemed to be that Southerners would not forgive such a statement when it came from a native Southerner. A week before the voting Stevenson appeared at a rally in the Florida panhandle near the Georgia border, where the emotional force of segregation was strongest, and was introduced by former Governor Millard Caldwell as "the most moderate man the South can elect." Caldwell then attacked Kefauver as "a sycophant of the Negro vote."[11] Stevenson later disclaimed responsibility for Caldwell's views, but, as Kefauver sharply pointed out, he took no counteraction.[12]

Stevenson won the primary, but by the narrow margin of

[8] *NYT*, Apr. 9.                    [9] *NYT*, May 13.
[10] *NYT*, May 15.                   [11] *NYT*, May 23.
[12] See Thomson and Shattuck, pp. 52-54.

about three percent of the vote. He ran well in areas where organized labor was strong and in Miami's Negro precincts. But he was also given heavy support by the Republican strong-holds and by the segregationist "wool hat" counties.

Throughout April and May, then, the primary campaigns steadily stoked the fires under the civil rights issue. Among the organizations that cherished the cause of civil rights, the pro-test against federal inaction became steadily more urgent. The segregationists' replies grew correspondingly sharper. The most dramatic conflict between them was their un-bridgeable difference over schools.

On May 17, the second anniversary of the Supreme Court's school decision, Negro and liberal organizations held rallies across the country. In New Orleans and four Alabama cities, White Citizens Councils held counter-rallies to mark "Black Monday." Senator Lehman declared that the race question should stand as a test for all election candidates. Governor Marvin Griffin of Georgia said in New Orleans that the Court decision "threatens to bring internecine strife never before seen in our country, and indeed menaces the very existence of this nation in the immediate future." Two hundred NAACP branches in thirty states held celebrations. The Rev. Martin Luther King, leader of the Negroes' bus boycott in Mont-gomery, Alabama preached to an audience of 12,000 at a thanksgiving service in the Protestant Episcopal Cathedral of St. John the Divine in New York City. The National Baptist Convention in the U.S.A., Inc., a Negro denomination, re-ported prayer services in 21 states.

Throughout the spring, NAACP leaders hammered at the issue's implications for the coming election. Two weeks after the administration's bill appeared, Thurgood Marshall warned that Negroes would cast their votes "solely" on the bases of the parties' respective performances on civil rights in Congress and of their platforms.[13] On April 24, two days later, 73 Ne-

[13] *NYT*, Apr. 23.

gro leaders convened in Washington to mobilize "moral and financial weight" in the fight for civil rights; they urged Negroes to support the NAACP and not to commit themselves to either party. This meeting was in response, not to the introduction of the administration's bills, but to the Southern Manifesto of March. In May Marshall declared on a television program that Negroes would support "the party that brings forth the best platform on civil rights and the best candidate on that question. Unless the Democratic party produces more than it has produced in the past, there is a possibility that some Negroes might vote Republican."[14] Later that week, before an audience of 16,000 in Madison Square Garden, Roy Wilkins, Executive Secretary of the NAACP, demanded that both parties adopt civil rights planks explicitly endorsing the Supreme Court's desegregation doctrine and promising to implement it.

The NAACP was aware that there were two competing explanations of Negro voting. One was racial and hinged on civil rights. The other was economic. Some Democratic leaders had argued that the Party's civil rights dilemma was far less dangerous than it appeared because the most important Negro voters were those living in the crowded working-class precincts of the big Northern cities. To these voters, civil rights was little more than an incomprehensible legal abstraction, the argument ran, and they would remain loyal to the Party of the New Deal and the Fair Deal, which had brought them economic security. To make their political influence felt, the Negro organizations faced the double necessity of attacking this view in Washington while working everywhere else to awaken their own followers to the importance of defending and expanding their legal rights.

The AFL-CIO announced in May a two million dollar fund drive to combat discrimination. George Meany, its President, was to head a new National Union Civil Rights Com-

[14] *NYT*, May 21.

mittee. He reflected a growing concern among labor officials that some Southern unions might secede rather than submit to their national headquarters' requirements that they desegregate their locals.[15] In the next two weeks broad anti-discrimination legislation was demanded by two big unions, the International Ladies Garment Workers and the Amalgamated Clothing Workers of America.

Later that month the American Jewish Congress urged both parties to pass a civil rights bill. On May 31, Robert W. Dowling, President of the National Urban League, an organization devoted to the improvement of Negroes' living conditions as they moved from Southern farms into the cities, announced the formation of Businessmen for Harriman; this group would stress Harriman's position on civil rights, particularly on desegregation of schools.

The Republicans did not hesitate to capitalize on the Democrats' difficulties. At a session of the National Citizens for Eisenhower, its press director, Richard L. Tobin, instructed an audience of party organizers to emphasize that "a vote for any Democrat is a vote for Eastland."[16]

## Two Supreme Court Decisions

The spring brought two Supreme Court decisions that were, from the Southerners' perspective, a tightening of the legal net in which they were enmeshed. A week before the administration's bills appeared, the Court handed down the *Nelson* decision, nullifying a Pennsylvania anti-subversion statute on grounds that congressional action in this field had pre-empted it for the federal jurisdiction. The implications for the states' rights doctrine were obvious. The *Richmond Times-Dispatch* protested on April 4 that the Court was ignoring the Constitution and again was indulging in outright legislation. J. Lindsay Almond, Attorney General of Virginia

[15] *NYT*, May 12.     [16] *NYT*, June 2.

and soon to be a candidate for governor, condemned this encroachment on the states' authority and demanded congressional counteraction.

Striking the racial issue directly, the Supreme Court ruled three weeks later that compulsory segregation in public transit was illegal and voided the South Carolina statute establishing it. In Alabama, the Montgomery City Bus Lines, hard hit by the Negroes' four-month boycott, immediately posted a notice in its garages announcing that segregation on its lines would end at five the next morning. Heavy political and public pressure was immediately brought to bear on the company, forcing it to revoke the order. In the midst of the furor, Eugene Cook, Attorney General of Georgia and one of its leading segregationist spokesmen, said he would recommend legislation making it a capital crime for any public official to assist the federal judiciary in enforcing the Supreme Court's desegregation rulings. The Governor could enforce racial segregation, he suggested, by calling out the National Guard as militia and declaring a limited state of martial law. The *Atlanta Constitution* commented on this proposal in a wry editorial on April 27 entitled: "We Need Sound Counsel, But We Have Mr. Cook."

There was, as usual, talk of a Southern third party movement, but most of it was confined to men around Governor George Bell Timmerman of South Carolina. Elsewhere, Southern politicians played down the idea, assessing more hopefully the chance of an accommodation at the convention.

The South's reaction to the Brownell bills was predictably adverse. In Virginia, the *Times-Dispatch* observed that they had appeared on the anniversary of Lee's surrender at Appomattox. Attorney General Almond charged that the bills were "specifically designed" to prevent states from adopting a pupil assignment plan, as Virginia was then contemplating. "Under pretense of solving this emotionally packed problem, the proposal would be used to prevent a state from endeavoring to evolve a solution consistent with the public welfare," he said. The proposed commission would constitute a "federal gestapo," he asserted, and its provision for utilizing volunteer assistance meant "the NAACP would provide such volunteers." Beyond that, he continued, "it would make the Attorney General legal counsel for a plaintiff at the cost of the American taxpayer. In effect, he would be chief counsel for the NAACP. He's almost that now."[17]

## The Congressional Atmosphere

In Congress that year the controversy over racial discrimination had not waited for the civil rights bills. It arose with the appearance of the President's program for federal aid to education, and it would not die down. Over the two sessions in which Congress wrestled with this civil rights program, the Southern strategy was reflected in the tone of the Southern oratory. As the Southerners' leaders gradually took control of the debate, putting the South's case in responsible hands and enforcing discipline, the quality of the speeches rose to an unusually high level, but the early Southern voices to be heard were those of visceral reaction and bitterly defensive.

On February 23, Representative Elijah Lewis Forrester of Leesburg, Georgia denounced the whole civil rights movement as Communist-inspired. "Tic" Forrester's Third District consisted of 24 counties, mostly rural and with a large Negro population.

> I could tell you for days and days wrongs that have been inflicted upon the white people of the South. . . . The Communist conspiracy was that the fight against us would be first waged on the grounds of equality, but denying that intermarriage and integration was sought or desired. That lasted only for a season. They are now demanding in unmistakable terms social equality and intermarriage. In fact, they are now contending that their race is the greatest in all history. . . .

[17] *Times-Dispatch*, Apr. 15.

Forrester addressed himself to the North and West:

I hope we are going to have your sympathy and your assistance. We do not wish to see the white gentile race disappear, and we do not intend for it to disappear. If you will sympathize with us now to the end that we shall have peace, I promise you that we will return that friendship and, if the struggle comes between godless communism and our form of government, that every Southerner will take his position in the ranks and give an account of his citizenship and loyalty that will be an inspiration to coming generations.

Of Forrester's discourse, Henderson L. Lanham of Rome, Georgia later said,

I commend my colleague for his splendid presentation of the position of the South. I wish that people of other sections of the country could realize just how difficult the problem is. I wish they could realize that we are not trying to keep the Negro in subservience; that we believe they should have all their legal rights; but we do object to the mingling of the races socially and in our schools because we know it is going to mean a mongrel race.[18]

Ezekiel C. Gathings of West Memphis, Arkansas, representing the First District and its heavily Negro counties along the Mississippi River, then put into the *Record* a series of reports from the files of the House Un-American Activities Committee on the leadership of the NAACP. They covered forty pages of fine print. "In 1954," Gathings summarized, "the total list of officers, board members, executive staff members, and others listed are 193. Out of that number, 89 of them have been cited by the House Un-American Activities Committee, or 46.1 percent of the total." He concluded, "The facts speak for themselves. . . . And I think that the Congress should probe this organization in all of its phases."[19]

It was into this atmosphere of rising congressional tempers,

[18] *Congressional Record*, 84th Cong., 2nd Sess. (hereafter *CR*), 3213 B. The letters A, B, and C refer to columns.
[19] *CR*, 3256 B, 3258 B.

and rising political stakes, that the administration's four civil rights bills fell.

## Clearance by the Judiciary Committee: Filibuster by Quorum Calls

As soon as the administration's bills were referred to the House Judiciary Committee, a vigorous four-sided struggle developed among: (1) the Committee Chairman, Emanuel Celler, Democrat of Brooklyn; (2) the bills' Republican advocates; (3) the conservatives who wanted no bills; (4) and liberals who demanded something substantially stronger. Celler's first reaction was to condemn the bills as "woefully lacking."[20] "It's like using a bean shooter when you should use a gun."[21] He preferred one of his own bills, H.R. 627, on which Judiciary's Subcommittee Number Two, chaired by Representative Thomas J. Lane of Lawrence, Massachusetts had held hearings the previous July. An omnibus bill, H.R. 627, included provisions similar to the administration's for a Commission and an additional Assistant Attorney General. It also contained extensive amendments to the old criminal statutes on civil rights and voting, as well as a prohibition against discrimination in interstate transportation. Its preamble was a forceful assertion that the rights of citizens were being denied, and a declaration that "it is essential to the national security and general welfare that this gap between principle and practice be closed."[22] But in introducing the administration's bills Keating warned, "If we try to bite off more than we can chew, Congress will get exactly nowhere—as in the past. . . . Let us not ruin the chance of success by an unrealistic approach to this serious national problem."[23]

[20] *Post*, Apr. 11.
[21] Associated Press dispatch printed in the *Constitution*, Apr. 11.
[22] This bill was reproduced in U.S. Cong., House, Subcommittee No. 5 of the Committee on the Judiciary, *Hearings on Civil Rights*, 85th Cong., 1st Sess., 1957, p. 270.
[23] *CR*, 6175 C.

Celler knew that without administration support H.R. 627 was not likely to go farther than any of its predecessors. Keating was aware that, without Chairman Celler's intervention, the Southerners could probably force interminable hearings on the new bills. Within a week a compromise was worked out: in Committee, the four administration bills would be substituted for the entire H.R. 627, which would retain its number and would continue to bear Celler's name as sponsor. As far as the rules were concerned, it would be the same bill on which hearings had already been held.

The Committee met in closed session on April 17, and the prearranged tactic was broken up immediately in an unexpected maneuver by its opponents. The motion to substitute was duly made, but before it came to a vote, Edwin E. Willis of St. Martinville, Louisiana moved to recommit the bill to Lane's Subcommittee. Willis' motion quickly passed by fourteen votes to thirteen. The successful coalition was composed of eight Southern Democrats, five Republicans, and Representative Francis E. Walter of Easton, Pennsylvania, a Democrat and Chairman of the Un-American Activities Committee.[24]

"If there had been the proper leadership by the administration we'd have had the bill out this morning," Celler said with irritation. But he added that to follow the usual procedure of referral to the Subcommittee would "enhance the chances of final passage, and the week's delay would be more than compensated for."[25] Celler asked Lane to hold a Subcommittee meeting the next day so that the bill could be reported back at the full Committee's next weekly meeting.

The next setback came from the proponents of the bill. When Lane's Subcommittee met, it insisted on Celler's original plan to substitute the administration language for the parallel sections of H.R. 627, but to retain all its further provisions. The NAACP praised the Subcommittee, but the Republicans

[24] *NYT*, Apr. 18; *Post*, Apr. 18.     [25] *NYT*, Apr. 18.

said they would cut the draft back in full Committee.

The full Committee met while the House was in session, and soon discovered itself the target of new harassment. The House convened at noon, and eleven minutes later a quorum call was demanded. The bells rang, and the Committee members ran for the elevators. In time they returned to the committee room. Then at 1.28 P.M. there was another quorum call. The third came at 2.05 P.M., and upon the fourth, at 2.55 P.M., Celler adjourned the Committee with nothing accomplished. The House adjourned shortly after. "A filibuster by quorum calls," Celler angrily called it; "these tactics have done no good. They are going to lose votes as a result." Keating charged that the effect was to "make clear that the weapon of delay will be used rather than an argument on the merits."[26] Celler immediately called another meeting for the following morning, before the House went into session. At this meeting the Committee cleared H.R. 627, with the administration's language substituted for all of Celler's.

The next step, before the bill could go to the floor, was to write the majority and minority reports. On April 25 Celler estimated that the reports would require a week or two. But the minority report did not appear until May 21, 26 days later, and the majority report the following day. The Southern minority culled the bill diligently for the ammunition it would need in the floor debates. The burden on the majority was even heavier, for a committee report was sometimes used by the courts in subsequent litigation to establish legislative intent. The Committee's staff was aware of the complexity of the legal issues raised by the bill and of the price that might be exacted for any serious misstatements in its exegesis.

## The Senate Hearings

During this hiatus in May, the Senate hearings ground along unproductively. It was generally assumed that the Senate

[26] *NYT*, Apr. 25; *Post*, Apr. 25.

Judiciary Committee would take no action whatever and intended nothing more than *pro forma* co-operation with the bill's sponsors, who had no choice but to await the eventual arrival of the House bill. The hearings' chief products were routine bickering and, on one occasion, a welcome touch of low comedy.

At the end of the day's hearings on May 16, Senator Olin Johnston of South Carolina was approached by Clarence Mitchell, head of the NAACP's Washington office and its chief lobbyist. Theodore Gaffney, a Negro photographer working for *Jet* magazine, photographed them in conversation. Johnston, who was up for re-election that year, reacted furiously. He declared Gaffney in violation of Senate rules and ordered guards to seize the film. Mitchell promptly charged that Gaffney was being treated in that fashion only because he was a Negro. After Gaffney had departed, the guards discovered that they had taken the wrong film from him. Johnston threatened to hold him in contempt if the pictures were published. Later a spokesman for *Jet* announced that the pictures had not come out.

## Hints of Dissension in the Administration

Uneasy about the President's equivocal support for the cause of civil rights, some of the liberal Democrats in the House anticipated charges that the administration program was the work of Brownell alone. Late in April James Roosevelt, a Los Angeles Democrat, wrote the President a letter emphasizing the need for Republican support in the Rules Committee. A week later Roosevelt read to the House the White House's reply, signed by the President's Administrative Assistant, Bryce N. Harlow:

> The President has asked me to assure you, respecting your April twenty-seventh letter, that the various civil rights measures proposed by the Attorney General were specifically approved by him prior to their submission to the

Congress, and it is, of course, the President's earnest desire that they be enacted into law. He specifically requested me to let you know of his confidence that the minority leaders will do all they appropriately can to ensure that this important legislation receives the serious consideration and prompt action it clearly deserves.

Any distinction between the two measures that Brownell had formally "proposed," and the two further measures that he had technically only asked Congress to consider, was imperceptible to the uninitiated.

But the hints of dissension within the administration persisted. On May 24 the President's "must list" appeared, enumerating the bills that he considered essential. Among the 28 bills were only two of the civil rights bills, those providing the Commission and the additional Assistant Attorney General. The enforcement sections were conspicuously absent. The list was handed to reporters by Murray Snyder, Assistant Press Secretary, who was immediately questioned on the omission. Snyder said the list contained the measures the President considered "necessary" in the current session and, without further elaboration, nonetheless made it obvious that there was no error. The *New York Times* added the next day, "A source at the Justice Department, who has been in close touch with the civil rights question, professed surprise and dismay at the change."

Brownell stuck to his guns. In a speech in Columbus to the Ohio Junior Chamber of Commerce on May 5, he had declared that the administration proposal "reflects the sincere and determined conviction that every person is entitled to be judged by what he alone is, and not by his race, color or religion." He had particularly emphasized the importance of the voting provisions. Even after the appearance of the "must list" and its portent of presidential displeasure, Brownell continued his campaign. On June 5 he addressed the National Press Club; calling for prompt congressional action, he warned that the nation must "face up to the ugly fact that

irresponsible action, left uncurbed, tends to get out of bounds.
. . . We must decide, quite particularly and openly, whether
to continue and encourage inhumanities and defiance of
law."[27] On June 6 Anthony Lewis commented in the *New
York Times* that "his words were regarded as the strongest
spoken thus far on the racial issue by any member of the administration."

## A Discharge Petition

The Judiciary Committee reported the bill to the House as
soon as the reports appeared, and it was referred to the Rules
Committee. The following week a bipartisan group of House
liberals announced they would soon open a drive for a discharge petition. On May 31 Representative Edith S. Green,
a Democrat from Portland, Oregon entered in the *Record*
a statement declaring the petition would be placed on the
clerk's desk June 5, to insure consideration by the House on
June 25. The statement was signed by twenty Democrats and
four Republicans.

Always a difficult and extraordinary device, the discharge
petition had of necessity become standard practice in handling
civil rights bills. Of the eight bills passed by the House in the
preceding two decades, six had been brought to the floor only
by discharging the Rules Committee. A seventh, a bill to outlaw the poll tax, had circumvented the Committee by a sus-
pension of the rules, a route that generally required the covert
collusion of the opponents. The eighth was the 1950 FEPC
bill, which came before the Committee while the short-lived
twenty-one-day rule was in effect. Under that rule, any bill
failing to receive a rule in that period could eventually be
brought to the House without one. The necessity of resort to
discharge generally indicated an intensity of opposition that,
at one stage or another, would prove fatal to the bill. Of 198
discharge petitions filed in the twenty years through 1956,

[27] United Press dispatch in the *Post*, June 5.

only twenty were successful. Of these twenty bills only one, the 1938 Wages and Hours Act, finally became law.[28]

In this case, the special nature of the Southerners' game made the discharge petition a somewhat more effective lever on them than usual. When a petition was signed by a majority of the House, it became in effect the rule for the bill, setting the length and conditions of the debate. If the opposition wished merely to do what it could to kill a bill, then often it put the petition to the test. But here the purpose of the opposition was to delay a bill that evidently commanded a substantial majority of the membership. To delay the bill as long as possible, it was necessary to control it as long as possible. As long as the bill followed the usual procedure, it was under the control of the Virginian who headed the Rules Committee, Howard Smith. But that would end as soon as a discharge petition went to the floor.

## The Effect of the California Primary

As the petition began to collect signatures, the Democratic primary campaign was coming to a dramatic climax on the other side of the continent. The fourth and decisive encounter between Stevenson and Kefauver was the California primary on June 5. With a strong liberal tradition and large Negro and Mexican-American minorities, California was extremely sensitive to the civil rights issue. Kefauver's manager, F. Joseph Donohue, charged: "The fact is that a vote for Stevenson is a vote for Eastland, Talmadge, Ellender and other white supremacy boys because the Stevenson bosses from Chicago have agreed to let them continue to control their political machines in their home states, while their hand-picked boy, Paul Butler, stays in power."[29] On June 3, in San Fran-

[28] Legislative Reference Service list prepared for Senator Knowland; and J. A. Robinson, *Decision-making in the Committee on Rules* (Ann Arbor: University Microfilm, 1958), p. 35.
[29] *Post,* June 2.

cisco, Kefauver openly suggested a deal between Stevenson and the Southern segregationists, under the terms of which racial desegregation was not to be pressed. On the same day, across the bay in Oakland, Stevenson said: "We will meet and master the crisis in civil rights. The Supreme Court has spoken the nation's conscience. . . ."

Stevenson carried the California Democratic primary election by nearly a two-to-one majority. The Negro precincts of San Francisco, Oakland, and especially Los Angeles supported him by majorities ranging from two-to-one up to four-to-one. The immediate effect of this triumph was to reduce markedly the emotional liberal pressure on Congress, for it demonstrated that the voters of a large urban state with a substantial Negro population would endorse Stevenson's reasoned and temperate approach to desegregation. As the news teletypes carried the voting figures eastward across the country, the adjective "moderate" lost its invective connotation. These figures did not affect the parties' imperative reasons for wanting to get the bill successfully through the House, but they suggested strongly that no election advantage was to be gained by staging a symbolic and foredoomed struggle among the Senate's intransigents.

The California primary effectively eliminated Kefauver from serious consideration, but four days later Governor Harriman formally announced his long-apparent candidacy. His declaration made it clear that the liberal pressure on Stevenson had not entirely ended. "We will win on the principle of civil rights that the Democratic party has always stood for," he told a hatters' union convention in New York City. He called for understanding of the "liberal men and women of the South," but went on to say: "The Republicans in the state have exposed the fact that all they want is a front for inaction, and I say to you, my friends, that these words— 'middle of the road' and 'moderation'—they mean only one thing. They are a front for inaction."

Harriman had miscalculated his timing. He was swiftly

plunged into the complexities of racial politics. Attempting to organize delegate strength in the West, he trapped himself in a series of embarrassments that must have delighted Stevenson's managers, as they began to enjoy a measure of success after the dreary months of attempting to reconcile the irreconcilables.

Democrats from twelve Western states were meeting to form a Harriman for President Committee with Governor Raymond Gary of Oklahoma, his chief Western supporter, as Chairman. As Harriman flew to meet them, Gary announced that the candidate had assured him that he would take a moderate approach "like Oklahoma" on the matter of schools. Landing in Denver, Harriman said uneasily that he would choose another adjective than "moderate." But he went on to explain that there was no difference in policy between Gary and himself. "Some scoundrels are trying to make me out the wild man on civil rights," Harriman complained. "That's simply not true." A *New York Times* reporter unkindly pointed out that, the day before in New York, Harriman had described himself as a zealot in the fight against discrimination. "I think Governor Gary has given a kind of leadership in his state that should be given on a nationwide basis," Harriman said. Gary explained that leadership by saying, "We are not exerting any pressure to bring about integration. . . . I'll admit that is moderation. But Governor Harriman believes, like I do, that if you leave people alone to work out this problem on a local level, they'll do it."[30]

## The President's Priorities

Dominated by the figure of the President, the Republican Party was much less concerned with the approaching convention. And the President was deeply preoccupied with an altogether different issue, the incessant struggle between the White House and Congress over foreign aid. President Eisen-

[30] *NYT*, June 17.

hower left no doubt that the mutual security appropriations were, in his view, the most urgently necessary bills before Congress. In early June the House repudiated a personal appeal from the President, and cut one billion dollars from his 4.9 billion dollar foreign aid request. The President's ileitis attack came the following day, and he was rapidly removed to Walter Reed Hospital for abdominal surgery early in the morning of June 9. Although he was not as desperately ill as he had been during his heart attack the previous September, he did not return to the White House for five weeks. In the interim his political activity was cut to the barest minimum. The day after the House finally passed its heavily cut foreign aid bill, Eisenhower sent a plea from his hospital bed for restoration of part of the money. Convalescing at his Gettysburg farm a month later, he announced that he would still run for a second term. But for any matter of less than critical importance, the invalid President had little strength.

## The Rules Committee and Representative Bolling

With the Republicans divided, the liberal Democrats managed to force the issue of civil rights in the Rules Committee on June 14. During a morning meeting convened for less incendiary matters, Richard Bolling of Kansas City, Missouri moved that the Committee go into closed session. With this, Bolling emerged publicly as the key to the padlock that was the Rules Committee. Bolling was then in his fourth term in Congress, and looked even younger than his forty years. A colleague described him as having the air of a junior faculty member at an expensive university. In the Rules Committee of 1956, his elders were apt to regard him as an impertinent youngster who required occasionally to be put in his place. But the Committee's deeply conservative majority had an even better reason to penalize Bolling whenever it could. Bolling already belonged to the small number of men who ran the House, and he was very close to Speaker Rayburn, with whom the majority of the Committee was constantly embroiled in one dispute or another. Bolling has been called a liberal who chose to be an operator rather than an orator.

As soon as Bolling made his motion for a session to vote on the school aid and civil rights legislation, William M. Colmer of Pascagoula, Mississippi began to deride him as "the new chairman." A congressman for 24 years, Colmer was the Committee's second-ranking Democrat. He called Bolling's motion "the most brazen action I have ever seen." Chairman Smith, who had also served twelve terms in Congress, complained that there was "no precedent" for voting on bills without hearings on them. The hearings were generally a matter of fifteen minutes, in which legislative committee chairmen and ranking minority members appeared to ask for time on the floor, but in rare instances, nearly always as a delaying device, extended testimony had been taken.

"You can run over me if you want to. You have the votes," Smith plaintively said. But he added, more ominously, that the Chairman has "privileges and perquisites," and these he promised to "exercise to the fullest extent."

Bolling insisted on a voting session that afternoon, and he got it. Overriding the Chairman, the Committee proceeded to clear the school bill and to schedule hearings on the civil rights bill. The vote on civil rights was six to four. The motion was supported by Bolling and three other Democrats, Ray J. Madden of Gary, Indiana; James J. Delaney of Long Island City, New York; and Thomas P. O'Neill of Cambridge, Massachusetts; as well as two Republicans, Clarence J. Brown of Blanchester, Ohio; and Harris Ellsworth of Roseburg, Oregon. The opponents were Smith, Colmer, James W. Trimble of Berryville, Arkansas, and the ranking Republican, Leo E. Allen of Galena, Illinois. Two members were absent. In the vote on the school aid bill, Allen supported the rule, but the alliances were otherwise the same.[31]

---

[31] Associated Press dispatch in the *Post*, June 15.

## Rules Committee Hearings

The hearings opened June 20 with Celler, the Chairman of the Judiciary Committee, as the first witness. Throughout the battle over this bill, Celler was conciliatory in his manner, accurate in his information, and honest in his answers. Celler's conduct of his case constituted one reason why the bill fared better in the House than in the Senate.

"If ever a time called for the harsh necessity of accommodating to changing climates, this is it," he began. " . . . I know how passionate these convictions are in certain sections of this country, and how this pattern has not been completely destroyed even in some of my sections of our country. . . ."[32] Questioned by Smith on the voting provisions, Celler explained they amended "that old Ku Klux Klan Act of 1870," a statute which, he said, had not been tested in sufficient court decisions to be fully defined.

> It was felt that if the Attorney General is privileged to bring suit, there will be probably greater determination by the courts as to what the meaning of these general terms is but they cover, I admit, Howard, they cover a pretty wide range of subjects and they could be made to stretch.

The testimony filled three days and contained the first version of the Southern counterattack on the bill.

"The time is very limited," Colmer told Celler, "but, as one of the long-time advocates of this type of legislation, I think you are entitled to a full hearing here and as far as I am concerned, I want to see that you get it."

"I understand those velvet words very well," Celler replied.

Colmer objected to the language permitting the Attorney General to act whenever he found persons "about to engage" in conspiracies to deprive others of their rights. Celler ob-

[32] U.S. Congress, House Committee on Rules, *Hearings before the Committee on Rules,* 84th. Cong., 2d Sess. On H.R. 627 (1956), p. 45 ff.

served that the phrase was not uncommon in injunction statutes. "Still a bit broad," Colmer suggested. He argued that
the bill attempted the impossible task of legislating social
values. ". . . You are trying to enforce the love of man for
man and you can't do it," he declared. He twitted Celler for
having accepted Republican language in substitute for his
own. Celler equably replied, "The only answer I can give to
that, I will say to the gentleman from Mississippi . . . is that
I am a good businessman. I will settle for half any time."

Allen, the Rules Committee's ranking Republican, said he
regretted that he was "not in sympathy" with his friend Celler
on the bill. "But," he added, "I have gone through this bill
and I cannot see where there is much wrong with it. . . .
As a matter of fact, I do not think anybody has to worry about
the bill itself." Ellsworth demanded reassurance on the "rather
unusual and very broad powers conferred upon the Attorney
General." Scott was cross-examined by Smith regarding the
Republican Party's support for the bill.

The opponents began to appear on the second day, and
Tic Forrester complained, "Had one fourth of the punitive
legislation been directed toward Communists and communism in this country that has been directed in this civil rights
legislation, you wouldn't have any Communists or communism in this country."[33] Willis objected that it was "inconsis-
tent" to ask, in the same bill, for both a Commission to study
new enforcement and the enforcement laws that the Commission was to study.

In the middle of Willis' testimony, Colmer interrupted to
point out that the Committee lacked a quorum. Only five
members were present: himself, Smith, Brown, Delaney, and
Bolling. Smith abruptly declared the meeting adjourned,
"subject to the call of the chair."

"Do I understand correctly that the chair intends to have a
further meeting this afternoon?" Bolling apprehensively
asked.

[33] *Ibid*, p. 101.

"It is not contemplated if the members don't have enough interest to come," Smith replied.

"There is a previous order of the Committee requiring the committee to act on this matter," Bolling protested. But the meeting was over. The effect was a delay of six precious days until the following Wednesday, June 27, when a petition of five Committee members forced the Chairman to continue with the hearings.

During those six days, it became increasingly evident that pressure from the White House was substantially restricting the Republicans' latitude in lending passive assistance to Smith's campaign of delay. There was a distinction to be drawn between the President as an individual and the White House as a large staff of men working in the President's name. Just as the inception of the administration bills followed the President's heart attack, so the administration's activity to push them through Congress followed his ileitis attack.

## The Rules Committee Votes

When the Rules Committee's hearings reconvened, it was apparent that the bill's supporters had the votes to move it. But the Southern congressmen were out in force to hold off the decision, and they talked for hours as the Committee listened. Colmer apologized to Willis for having interrupted him the week before, "but the boys were playing a little rough around here and we played a little rough along with them."

William M. Tuck of South Boston, Virginia embarked on a review of the Reconstruction years. "Shortly after the War Between the States—am I taking up too much time, sir?"

"I am enjoying your remarks," Smith blandly replied.

"Thank you, sir. Shortly after the War Between the States. . . ," and Tuck proceeded at length.

George M. Grant of Troy, Alabama charged that the bill was written precisely for the purpose of implementing the school desegregation decisions. Robert T. Ashmore of Greenville, South Carolina asserted it attacked "the rights of the individual" and concentrated still more power in the central government.

But finally Smith said to the crowd of waiting witnesses, "See if you can't get together and shorten your testimony. I haven't encouraged any shortening in the past, but the jig's up. I know it."[34]

At five o'clock, Bolling made a motion for executive session. "Mr. Chairman, is that motion debatable?" Colmer asked. "Debate it," said Smith.

Colmer observed that about a dozen congressmen were still waiting to be heard. "This is not an unprecedented action," Bolling argued. "The House itself limits debate." He moved the previous question, and apparently only Colmer opposed it.

Allen said, somewhat apologetically, "Mr. Chairman, we want to give you an opportunity on the floor. If anyone has an idea how much debate, I will go along with plenty of hours for debate." John Bell Williams of Raymond, Mississippi quipped, "I'd say two or three months."[35] With that, the Committee retired to vote in privacy.

A rule was granted, eight to three. The four Northern Democrats and the four Republicans supported it. Three of the Southerners opposed it; the fourth, Homer Thornberry of Texas, was not present.

The rule itself was the standard form.[36] It called for two days' debate, with time divided between the Chairman of the Judiciary Committee and the ranking Republican, to be followed by amendments under the five-minute rule. The length of the debate was not unprecedented, although it was unusual. Rules generally called for one or two hours' debate.[37] One

[34] *NYT*, June 28. This remark does not appear in the published record of the hearings.
[35] *Rules Committee Hearings*, p. 149.
[36] *House Resolution 568*, 84th Cong., 2d Sess.
[37] Robinson, p. 35. This total does not include closed rules.

other open rule in that Congress had called for two days, and in the preceding eight Congresses there had been thirteen rules for two days of debate and one for three days.

In any case, the length of the debate was merely a concession by the winners to the losers. The bill was over its second and most dangerous hurdle. The Democratic leadership had made it clear that the bill would be allowed to come to the floor in routine fashion, and there the outcome was hardly in doubt. If it came too late to permit Senate action, that was a matter of concern mainly to a rather small number of the most deeply committed advocates of civil rights legislation. The one great task remaining for the bill's supporters in the House was to see it to passage with its reputation undamaged by the debates and its effectiveness uncompromised by amendment.

## The Relationship of the School Aid Bill

The struggle over the school aid bill was the prelude to the civil rights debate on the floor. No bill travels through Congress alone. To the Southerners, and to many Northern liberals, the two bills were only different facets of the same federal assault upon Southern school segregation. Southern congressmen feared, with substantial reason, that federal subsidy to their school systems might eventually be turned into an economic lever to force compliance with the desegregation decisions. The law on this point was as unsettled as on every point in the field of racial relations; whatever the intentions of Congress, the allocations of federal money might be subject to possible court decisions or administration rulings in the future. Some Northern Democrats, under the leadership of Harlem's Adam Clayton Powell, were determined to write language into the school aid bill to insure that no funds would go to segregated systems. Other Northern Democrats, whose spokesman was Lee Metcalf of Helena, Montana, sought to head off Powell's amendment with the argument that federal aid to segregated systems was unconstitutional under existing law. The dispute developed months before the administration's civil rights program appeared.

President Eisenhower sent his bill for federal aid to education up to Congress on January 12. Within two weeks Powell announced that he would again force a vote on his amendment, a technique that had already been responsible for the defeat of earlier attempts to pass school aid legislation.

Powell charged in a speech on the floor on January 24:

> The only reply I get is, "Your amendment might kill the bill." How shocking that we Americans, who are supposedly religious, have so lost our sense of values that we are willing to support illegal and immoral un-American actions and attitudes. But I have refused to be dissuaded, to retreat, to compromise. Unless the grace and truth of the prophets and Jesus Christ supersede the mores and customs of bigotry, our nation will never be exalted.

Metcalf replied, early in February, that the Powell amendment would set an unwholesome precedent by implying that funds to openly defiant states could be cut off only where Congress specifically required it. "I do not believe that is the law and I will not vote for an amendment that concedes it to be the law," he said. Some states were earnestly beginning to comply with the decisions, he pointed out, and there the Powell prohibition would be "a deterrent to the very gradualism that the Supreme Court desires." As for the hard core of intransigent states, he continued, the administration was shirking its clear duty in its refusal to cut off the federal aid their schools already enjoyed through the school lunch program and other direct subsidies.[38] Metcalf was a former associate justice of the Montana Supreme Court, and his legal opinions carried more than the usual weight.

In the course of the next months, the Education and Labor Committee rejected the Eisenhower proposals and wrote a much broader bill (H.R. 7535) to be sponsored by the

[38] *CR*, 2119 A to 2120 A.

Committee's second-ranking Democrat, Augustine B. Kelley of Greensburg, Pennsylvania. The Kelley bill came to the floor at the end of June. The timing was fatal. The bill's supporters had hoped the civil rights votes would be taken earlier in the session. The main threat to school aid was the Powell amendment, and it could have been defeated only if liberal House members had been given an earlier opportunity to go on record for the more comprehensive administration civil rights program. As it happened, the liberals were under the pressures of the coming election, and few of them cared to risk a vote against Powell with the civil rights roll calls still in the future and uncertain. It was the conservative majority in the Rules Committee that was responsible for the order in which the two bills went to the floor.

As the debate on the Kelley bill opened, Colmer immediately put Metcalf's legal argument to his own use. He declared that the outcome of Powell's campaign was irrelevant, since an embargo on aid to segregated schools could be imposed by administrative action whether or not Congress insisted on it.[39] The Eisenhower administration had flatly told the NAACP some months before that it would not adopt that policy unless the courts forced the issue upon it.[40] But both Colmer and Metcalf pointed to a ruling on April 6 by the Civil Aeronautics Administration that had cut off federal funds for airport terminals that were to be segregated.[41] From this ruling the two men drew opposite inferences.

"Is not the conclusion inescapable," Colmer asked, "that the states maintaining segregation in their public schools are going to be taxed without receiving any of their tax money back from the Federal Government to help construct their own schools? Make no mistake about it, the people of those states

[39] *CR*, 11298 A.
[40] Letter from Harold C. Hunt, Undersecretary of Health, Education and Welfare, to Clarence Mitchell, Washington representative of the NAACP, Dec. 20, 1955. This letter was read into the *Congressional Record* by Powell on Feb. 6, 1956, at 1192 B.
[41] Civil Aeronautics Administration, *Airport Policy and Procedure Memorandum 41*, Apr. 6, 1956.

are going to have segregated schools as long as they have public schools."[42] Metcalf called it "an unfortunate coincidence" that the segregation controversy was being imposed upon the question of school aid. "The Powell amendment is not needed; it should not be put in this legislation," he said. Because it demanded immediate compliance where the Supreme Court had only required "all deliberate speed" toward desegregation, Metcalf asserted that the amendment amounted to "repudiation" of the Court.[43]

Much more profoundly than the civil rights fight, the debates on school aid illustrated the painfully ambivalent feelings of most Southern congressmen toward the towering power of the federal government. In any discussion of civil rights alone, the federal government appeared only in its role as policeman and social reformer; this the Southerners resented hotly and almost unanimously. But there was another side to the federal authority. With its formidable treasury it had brought many good things to the nation's least wealthy region, things that the South's citizens could never have afforded for themselves.

Colmer represented not only the extreme position on the race question but the adamantly conservative view on all social and economic legislation. The two did not invariably accompany each other. A great many Southerners were convinced liberals on every subject but racial relations. Colmer was playing the Southern conservative's traditional game of using the overheated racial issue to undercut Southern liberalism on social legislation. The Southern congressman's dilemma, one of the great tragedies of the endlessly complicated politics of black and white, was revealed with crystalline clarity in an earnest speech on the floor by Henderson L. Lanham of Rome, Georgia.

When I was elected to Congress, one of the things I promised the people of my state was that I would do my best to secure Federal aid for our schools. I am convinced that it is one of

[42] *CR*, 11298 B.   [43] *CR*, 11460 B.

the obligations of the Federal Government to help those states which are unable because of the limitation of their resources to furnish school buildings and educational facilities for their children. It has always seemed to me that money should be taken where it can be found and spent where it is needed in the field of education.

Lanham pointed out that he had helped pass the laws, prototypes of general school aid, that provided subsidies for school districts burdened with children whose parents were employed by large tax-exempt federal installations. He concluded:

> But when an effort is made to bribe my state and the South with school construction money to accept the mixing of the races in our schools, I cannot vote for a bill so designed. The South does not intend to mix the races in the schools because it believes that to do so would be to break down the social barriers which at present prevent the temptation to intermarriage of the two races. This fear of intermarriage which would destroy both races and result in a race of halfbreeds and mongrels is the basic reason for the South's fight against integration in the schools.[44]

Powell introduced his amendment on July 3, declaring, in the face of a great deal of experience to the contrary, "This bill is going to pass the House if the Powell amendment is in it. How will it kill the bill?"

He did not have to wait more than a few minutes for his answer. The opponents' strategy was immediately apparent. The speaker to follow Powell was Stuyvesant Wainwright, a Republican from Wainscott, Long Island. He was against the bill but, significantly, he was for the amendment. Wainwright conceded that he had introduced the administration's school bill at the request of the Secretary of Health, Education and Welfare. "Then we had four months of testimony, and I changed my mind." He charged that the centralization of education carried a threat of totalitarian government, but he

[44] CR, 11457 A-B.

went on to give the Powell amendment a hearty endorsement.

Powell asked uneasily whether Wainwright would support the bill if the Powell amendment were written into it. Wainwright replied:

> If the Powell Amendment is agreed to and provided the basic changes requiring the states to amend their ways, I will support the bill. I will support it, not believing in Federal aid to education, but only to show my sincere support of the gentleman's motion. In other words, it will show that I believe the greater question to be the principle of a nation of great civil rights.[45]

The genuine supporters of school aid, men of both parties, quickly reiterated their warnings that the amendment would destroy the bill. Bolling introduced a letter from former President Truman to that effect. Peter Frelinghuysen, a Republican from Morristown, New Jersey asserted that a vote for the amendment was a vote against the bill; caught in the middle of the cross fire, Frelinghuysen was leading a losing attempt to scale the Democrats' bill down to the administration's intention on one hand and yet to beat off the Powell campaign on the other.

Powell's ally, James Roosevelt, said, ". . . I do not believe that any legislative body has the right to give public funds to those who are in open defiance of the Supreme Court of the United States." But Cleveland M. Bailey, Democrat of Clarksburg, West Virginia, an old and ardent advocate of school aid, retorted that Powell "is not satisfied with equality; he wants the Congress to give special treatment to his race. He wants us to . . . pass legislation to punish somebody. It is not the purpose of the Congress of the United States, it is not the function of the Congress, to pass punitive legislation. . . ."[46] The phrase frequently recurred in the speeches of Democrats attempting to mollify the enmity between the extreme factions of their Party on the matter of Negroes' rights.

[45] CR, 11758 A.  [46] CR, 11761 A-B.

The debate reached a dramatic climax when William L. Dawson took the floor to oppose the amendment. Dawson had been in Congress longer than either of the other two Negro members, Powell and Charles C. Diggs of Detroit. Dawson's background differed considerably from Powell's. Soft spoken and undemonstrative, Dawson was born in Albany, Georgia and went first to the Normal School there and then to Fisk University, a Negro institution in Nashville. Later he went North to begin law school and his long rise through Chicago's ward politics. Powell was born in New Haven, Connecticut and took degrees at Colgate and Columbia before he went into the ministry. His political career lay in liberal causes and Negro movements, while Dawson's was in the regular Democratic organization. A striking figure, tall and well-tailored, Powell was said to have a taste for fast cars and public controversy. He had combined politics with his post as minister of Harlem's big Abyssinian Baptist Church. A sophisticate and widely traveled, he was at that time married to Hazel Scott, the jazz pianist. Dawson directed the House Government Operations Committee, of which he was Chairman, with a steady-handed caution; he has never attempted to share the spectacular publicity that occasionally accrued to his subcommittee chairmen in their investigations. The mercurial Powell seldom concerned himself with the routine mechanics of running Congress, and in 1956 he had run up one of the highest records of absence from the floor of the House.

"More than seventy years ago I was born in the South," Dawson told the House.

When I was a child, the school for the colored kids was open only a few months out of the year, when they didn't need us in the fields. Sometimes those who were engaged to teach could barely read and write themselves. The schools for others were open nine months out of the year, with adequate schoolrooms and with adequate facilities and with trained teachers. [He was able to go to a private school because his mother and grandmother worked to send him there.] I recite these things to you to let you know that I know something about America. I know something about the system, but I believe in America and I believe in our institutions. That is why I am opposing the Powell amendment. . . . A national crisis now faces this nation of ours and schoolrooms are needed by all the children of America. . . . The education of the young is as fundamental for the preservation of this nation of ours as maintaining a standing army. . . .

Oh, I remember when a member of my race could not vote in the South. We could not vote in the South because the Republican party would not run any candidates for election and the Democratic party ran under the white primary. Therefore, Negroes were foreclosed from the polls. But, the Supreme Court issued an edict that since the Democratic primary is the only method of expressing yourself in Federal elections, you could not keep them out of the Democratic primary. And that is why we have had a chance in the South to go forward in spite of the iniquitous agreement entered into by both parties. Go back and read the record. . . .

I am of the opinion that the Supreme Court has adequate powers to enforce its decisions. This amendment can add nothing to its powers. Nothing can be done under this amendment unless and until the Court rules a State or school district is in contempt; when that occurs the Court will decide and impose the necessary penalties, and it becomes the duty of the Executive to carry out those orders.[47]

The liberals in the House were deeply divided over the question. When the Powell amendment came to a vote, late that afternoon, it passed by a margin of 164 to 116. It was a teller vote, but it was clear that heavy support came from Republican conservatives who opposed the principle of federal aid to education. And many Southerners had left the floor to avoid voting against the amendment.

The House took a holiday on July 4 and came back the next day to finish the job. The turmoil over amendments be-

[47] CR, 11763 C to 11764 A.

came ludicrous when the Powell forces, resting on their victory, grew inattentive and suffered a damaging defeat. It revolved around what appeared to be a purely fiscal amendment introduced by Ralph W. Gwinn, a conservative Republican from New York's well-to-do, suburban Westchester County. As a substitute for the bill's complex distribution formula for aiding most heavily the poorest school districts, Gwinn proposed the simple device of returning to each state one percent of the federal income taxes collected there. This kind of amendment had been a standard fixture in federal aid debates, and it was usually borne to an early and certain demise. In this instance, miraculously, the Gwinn amendment passed on tellers, 122 to 120.

Some minutes passed before the Powell people realized what had happened. In agitation Roosevelt rose to point out that the Gwinn amendment had struck the first ten pages of the bill, carrying with it not only the distribution formula but, incidentally, the Powell amendment as well. Under the rules the vote on the Gwinn amendment could be repeated when the Committee of the Whole reported the bill back to the House. But there would be no further opportunity to replace the Powell language in those pages.

Powell reappeared with a hastily-drafted second version of his amendment, to be written into the part of the bill still subject to change. He now put forward a new title declaring "that there shall be no Federal funds allotted or transferred to any state which fails to comply with the provisions of the Supreme Court." The lawyers in the House pounced on the vagueness of the language. A substitute was hastily patched together by an unlikely alliance of Roosevelt, Keating, and Charles A. Halleck of Rensselaer, Indiana, and it passed by 177 votes to 123.

The Committee of the Whole then rose, the Speaker and the mace returned to the rostrum, and the final votes were taken. The Gwinn amendment, having served its purpose, was thrown out. The new Powell amendment was passed, although, now that the voting was being recorded, by a narrower margin: 225 to 192. At last the role was called on the school aid bill itself. It failed, 192 to 224, with the majority largely supplied by Southerners and Republicans.

This defeat was owed to the 95 members who had voted for the Powell amendment and then turned around to oppose the bill. They were all Republicans, nearly two-thirds of them from the Middle West. Among them, violating his promise to Powell, was Wainwright. The strategy had worked. Republican votes for the amendment had insured Southern votes against the bill.

## Rule XXII and the Civil Rights Bill

The opposition to the civil rights bill enjoyed fewer opportunities. The bill involved only one political issue, rather than two that could be played off against each other. The Democratic leadership had accepted the administration's draft, effectively discouraging organized Republican attacks on it. As the session swung through June into July, the Southern tactic of delay turned into a narrow calculation of days remaining.

Under Rule XXII, the Rules Committee must present a rule to the House within three legislative days; the rule then goes to the calendar. "Only the member designated by the Committee on Rules may call up the rule the first seven days on the calendar," according to *Cannon's Procedure*. After that it may be called up by any member, although in practice the leadership schedules floor action.

Chairman Smith had designated Colmer to handle the rule. He reported it on the third day, July 2, and proceeded to wait out the seven additional days and whatever further grace might be extended by the leadership. "I'm not going to rush them," he told Frank Van der Linden of the *Richmond Times-Dispatch*. "Time is of the essence. We have delayed this bill all year." Another Southerner told Van der Linden,

"We will try to bring up as many amendments as we can to take up time."[48]

The seventh legislative day after July 2 was July 11, a Wednesday. But during the first week of July the leadership had scheduled the bill for Monday, July 16. It was usually considered wise to take up controversial business at the beginning of the week, since there was apt to be diminished attendance as the weekend approached.

## Another Southern Manifesto

In the meantime, the Southerners drew up another Manifesto pledging themselves once again to use every available legal resource against the civil rights bill. Bearing a strong resemblance to the March Manifesto, it charged that the bill violated states' rights, effected further concentration of federal power, gave the Attorney General unprecedented authority, and increased racial discord. Heralding it with unconcealed enthusiasm, the *Richmond Times-Dispatch* observed that of three North Carolina congressmen refusing to sign the March Manifesto, two had been defeated in the spring primary. In spite of this warning, the Southern support of the new Manifesto was not quite unanimous. It did not carry the names of one congressman from Florida, two from Tennessee, three from North Carolina, or fourteen from Texas. Speaker Rayburn had been "visibly angered" by it, the *Times-Dispatch* reported, and had counseled the Texas delegation to avoid it.[49] On the day the Manifesto appeared, Federal Judge John Paul ordered public school officials in Charlottesville, Virginia, the seat of the University of Virginia, to present plans for the beginning of integration the following September. Attorney General Almond himself was representing the state in the case, and former Governor John S. Battle, the school board.

[48] *Times-Dispatch*, July 8.          [49] *Times-Dispatch*, July 12.

In Gettysburg the President was convalescing at his farm, and congressional leaders called on him to work out a program for the last weeks before adjournment. After the meeting they reported that he felt most strongly about the foreign aid appropriations, which faced trouble in both houses of Congress. A list of fourteen measures was drawn up at this conference, and it included, of the various civil rights proposals, only the Commission. Senator Styles Bridges of New Hampshire, Chairman of the Republican Policy Committee, quoted the President as having said he had asked for "very little" in the way of civil rights legislation, but that little he expected to get. The Democratic leaders were less sanguine. They did not even include the Commission on their list of possibilities.[50]

For the first time since his ileitis attack five weeks earlier, the President returned to the White House on Sunday, July 15, the day before the House began to debate the civil rights bill. By this time it was clear that the congressional leadership hoped to adjourn by July 29, and the bill's death in the Senate was more of a foregone conclusion than ever.

## House Debate on the Rule

On Monday afternoon, Colmer called up the rule for the civil rights debate. He did it with "the greatest reluctance," and he took some pains to explain why he found himself managing the rule for a bill of which the Sixth District of Mississippi disapproved so heartily. "With complete frankness," he told the House, "I reported this out to the House some weeks ago for the simple reason that I desired to control its consideration and delay the proposed legislation as long as possible." He took the opportunity to expound his view of the Negro and his progress in this country:

> This progress has been accomplished under the leadership of his white friends, chiefly his Southern white brother. We in the South are proud of this progress, and we hope for its

[50] *NYT*, July 11.

orderly continuation. But it must be realized that it is impossible by legislative enactment or judicial decree to place overnight a race of people, who until a few generations ago were unenlightened human beings, running wild in the jungles of Africa, on an equal plane with another race of people who for thousands of years have enjoyed the benefits of civilization, education, culture, and Christianity.[51]

Colmer's answer to the bill's voting section was blunt: it was best to let the white man do most of the South's voting for the time being. The case was rarely put so explicitly.

Under the House's procedures, the first question was whether it wished to adopt the rule and debate the bill. Calling for a "full length" debate, Smith proposed amending the rule to provide eight hours' time instead of two days'.

"Let us assume the amendment is agreed to," replied the canny Celler, "and we have eight hours of general debate. Let us assume also—I do not know that this will be so—that there will be continued quorum calls at the opening of the session tomorrow. Does this mean that the eight hours would continue after the quorum calls or any other efforts on the part of those in opposition to the bill to obstruct orderly procedure?" (Quorum calls were not counted against debating time.)

Smith urbanely suggested that the bill was "of such transcendent importance" that it seemed to him a quorum ought to be present. Halleck cut in to say bluntly, "Of course, I think all of us should understand that if two days is changed to eight hours, we will be here a great deal longer."

## The House Begins to Debate the Civil Rights Bill

The trap had been spotted, and Smith's amendment was voted down 103 to 151. The rule was passed, and the House resolved itself into the Committee of the Whole to consider H.R. 627. The time was controlled by Celler, as Judiciary

[51] CR, 12917 B.

Committee Chairman, and Keating, as ranking minority member, with each to allocate half. Because both were on the same side of the issue, the bill's opponents had to come to its supporters for opportunity to speak.

Celler opened in his customary conciliatory tone.

> Mr. Chairman, if ever a time called for the harsh necessity of accommodating to changing climates, this is it. Much as I openly and vigorously fought for civil rights originally which would go far beyond those proposals now before you, I recognize and have always recognized the difficulty of adjustment faced by those who as vigorously as I support these measures equally vigorously oppose them. Concepts change slowly and not without tragic tensions.

Then he answered Colmer:

> We cannot maintain for long the concept of aristocracy of one color against another. The inevitability of the destruction of such patterns must be acknowledged. And I say this in all solemnity lest with tensions high and bitterness mounting, we invite the spread of cruel antagonisms. Ultimately, the same results will emerge that could have emerged without the bitterness and hatred that is now being engendered.

The South's spokesmen took a different view. They were well prepared for this moment and proceeded to make the most of their opportunity. Celler and Keating let them do most of the talking. The Southerners' attack went immediately to the main points of their case. In the first twenty minutes of the debate, they leveled at the bill all of the three accusations that were to win the South's victories the following year. In 1957 these three points would catch the bill's supporters by surprise. The administration and the newspapers, as well as the Senate liberal leaders, had fallen into the dangerous habit of dismissing Southern oratory on this kind of bill as mere windy logic-chopping. The warning lay before the bill's supporters, and they generally ignored it.

First, the Southerners charged that the bill was intended to give the Attorney General the authority to initiate school desegregation suits. Second, they charged that its procedures were designed to eliminate the right of jury trial for defendants accused of violating Negroes' rights. And third, the Southerners questioned whether this bill had the support of the President. None of these issues was developed subtly; all were mixed in with much bombast, doubtful sociology, and miscellaneous grievance that became less important later in the bill's career. All of this, the significant with the trivial, was dismissed by the liberals outside the House as merely the traditional ritual of another Southern political Thermopylae.

The school question was first raised on the floor by a Republican, William L. Springer of Champaign, Illinois. Keating returned a vague answer and retired to confer with counsel. A few minutes later it was raised again by a liberal Democrat, Sidney R. Yates of Chicago: ". . . would not the gentleman say that this bill would give the right to the Attorney General to implement the Supreme Court decisions?"

Celler replied, "In my humble judgment, I would. Let us be fair about it, because that old statute covers all filching [sic; this word is clearly a shorthand reporter's misunderstanding of *fashion*] of constitutional rights, no matter what those rights may be. It covers all phases of American life. Let us be frank about it."

Smith immediately picked up the point. "Let us say," he began, "that little Rastus down in Georgia wants to go to a white school and he asks to go to a white school and they tell him no. Then he goes on about his business and goes to a colored school, where he will be happier and learn more. Then the NAACP goes to the Attorney General. May the Attorney General bring suit whether Rastus wants to or not?"

"I think he could," Celler replied. Keating agreed, with the qualification that the Attorney General could act only where there was a conspiracy to deny a citizen his rights. He and Celler pointed out that the existing statute gave a Negro parent, for example, the right to recover damages from members of a school board that violated his child's rights by refusing to accord him a place in a nonsegregated school. The enforcement sections of the bill authorized the Attorney General to bring, in a citizen's behalf, civil rights suits that the citizen was already empowered to bring in his own behalf. William A. Winstead of Philadelphia, Mississippi concluded: "Sponsors of this legislation do not disguise the fact that this legislation is intended to implement the recent Supreme Court decisions in the school segregation cases."

George W. Andrews of Union Springs, Alabama asked: "Is it a correct statement to say, then, that the difference between existing law and the bill before the House is that under the bill before the House the Government would furnish a lawyer from the Attorney General's office to an aggrieved party?"

"The gentleman can put it that way if he wishes," Celler replied evenly. "I would rather say that the Attorney General could intervene."[52]

## Absence of Trial by Jury

The jury trial issue had been opened by Colmer as soon as he reported the rule. "And bear in mind," he warned, "that the bill further provides for the trial of these cases in the Federal courts, without the benefit of trial by jury. It does not require much imagination to see what would happen if an unscrupulous and politically-minded person became head of this [Justice] Department."[53]

"I tell you it is a most dangerous piece of legislation," declared South Carolina's Ashmore later that day. "Let no one in this chamber forget, let no one fail to remember, that you do not get a trial by jury in a case of this kind. Ask any lawyer in this Congress and let him tell you what this bill does. You are deprived of the right of trial by jury under an

[52] *CR*, 12923 B to 12927 A.  [53] *CR*, 12918 A.

injunction proceeding that is set forth in this act. Is that what you want?"

W. R. Poage of Waco, Texas argued that the best protection of minority rights lay in the English common law as the United States Constitution guaranteed it. "Basic in these guarantees is a right of trial by jury," he said. "This bill substitutes for the right of the accused to demand a jury the right of the Attorney General to get a Federal court injunction, whether the party who is supposed to be about to suffer wants the injunction or not."

"This bill tampers with, and in many cases abolishes, the right to trial by jury," repeated L. Mendel Rivers of Charleston, South Carolina. "It is strange indeed that a bill which purports to be a civil rights bill would molest one of the greatest, if not the most basic, element of our civil rights— the right of trial by jury." He noted that the bill was limited to civil remedies. "But it is quite obvious to me, and I think it should be to any lawyer, that this is mere subterfuge—and that what we are really asked to do is to provide for criminal prosecutions in the guise of civil actions for redress."

None of the Southerners spelled out this charge in detail. Jury trial in contempt proceedings is a highly technical matter, and it was not argued in any detail until the following year. But the bill's supporters in the House understood the accusation. One incautious liberal member lent a measure of substance to it in the very baldness of his reply. Roosevelt retorted: "Criminal proceedings in the field of civil rights have been highly ineffectual. Local sentiment has made jury convictions almost impossible."[54]

## The Position of the President

The precise nature of the President's endorsement of the bill continued to be the subject of much Southern interest. Keating said at the beginning of the debate:

[54] *CR*, 13158 A to 13180.

I do want to impress upon my colleagues on both sides of the aisle that the bill before us is line by line and word for word, one of the key measures of President Eisenhower's program. . . . This proposal epitomizes the philosophy of President Eisenhower in his administration in approaching the thorny problems which exist in this field.

Martin Dies of Lufkin, Texas continued to have doubts.

The gentleman made the statement that this is a legislative measure of the Eisenhower program. I had understood that all the President recommended was the establishment of a commission. Do I understand and do the people of Texas understand that this bill is the bill that President Eisenhower wants enacted?

"This bill is the bill which President Eisenhower wants enacted, and I can say that to the gentleman without any question," Keating replied.

"There is no message before us," Dies pointed out. "I want to clear this up."

"I would be glad to explain exactly what took place," Keating replied. "The gentleman is quite right that no special message on this bill is before us. The Attorney General appeared before us and asked for Parts I and II of this bill and said that he had in mind doing the other things later. After that when the committee got into it the Attorney General sent to us the wording for Parts III and IV. I can say to the gentleman unqualifiedly, therefore, what I did say— that this is word for word in accordance with the Administration's ideas."

"The gentleman is talking about Brownell," Dies objected. "I am talking about President Eisenhower. Has he ever supported this bill? Has he ever stated to the gentleman or anyone else that he is in favor of it?"

"I am informed that President Eisenhower and his Administration favor this bill which is before us today," Keating tersely answered, ending the exchange.[55]

[55] CR, 12918 B to 12919 B.

## Loose Terminology

The loose terminology of the bill was another matter repeatedly raised by the opposition, which charged that its scope was unduly broad and vague. A Republican, Noah M. Mason of Oglesby, Illinois, interrupted Smith to say, "The question is this: Is not Title III a general title that would cover labor rights, religious rights, school rights, as well as every other kind of rights?"

"That is true," Smith replied,[56] and Celler agreed.

"What is 'unwarranted economic pressure'?" asked Willis, from St. Martinville, Louisiana, reading from the list of subjects to be investigated by the proposed commission. "What is 'economic, social and legal developments'? No one knows, it is not defined in the bill." He observed that the term "economic pressure" might involve the regulation of labor unions.[57]

The South spoke with many voices. It was a punitive bill; it was a sectional bill; it was a Communist conspiracy; it attempted the impossibility of legislating social usage; it interfered with the order in which the Lord meant the various races to live. The poignant overtones of nostalgia were clearly audible when Representative Tuck said, "We yearn for the return of the halcyon days that we have known and for a restoration of the peace and tranquility which has heretofore been so characteristic of our people."

The bill, they said, contained in the proposed Commission an attempt to harass by investigation. Martin Dies recalled the liberal attacks on his memorable stewardship of the Un-American Activities Committee: "What has happened to the liberals? Have you disappeared, or have you embraced the doctrine that the end justifies the means?" The sally passed unanswered, but it foreshadowed the devastating barrage that would be brought to bear by the South the following year on the older liberals who remembered the days when the injunction was anathema to their cause.

[56] CR, 12922 A.                    [57] CR, 13140 A-B, 13144 B-C.

The main defense was a technical matter, left to Celler and Keating. There were many speeches for the record, referring to the great cause of equal rights and the nation's image abroad. Congressman Diggs complained that, to avoid the inevitable "inflammatory reaction," the bill's advocates had failed to recite the South's long record of violations of voting rights, the substantial issue that lay behind the technicalities of Part IV.

Powell leaped briefly into the fight with a broad barrage of assertions that damaged his allies as much as his opponents.

> This legislation comes much too late. It is too weak for the job that should be done and carries in its language dangerous loopholes which could be used in the wrong hands to hurt those whom we are trying to help. . . . It is a known fact to those of us on the inside that this particular bill, in its completed form, has been in the hands of the Justice Department for many months. Discussions concerning it took place early last year. If this bill had been sent over when it was completed we would have ample time to have discussed it, passed it, and sent it to the Senate. . . .

Powell suggested that the phrase "economic pressure" might permit it to be used against the Montgomery bus boycott. Noting that the bill would give the Justice Department authority to act when persons were "about to engage" in unlawful activities, he asked, slipping strangely into the Southern argument, "Is this not a form of thought control, a dangerous power to give to any Attorney General of the United States regardless of who he may be?" He did not seem reassured by Keating's careful explanations. The bill's supporters hastily got a letter from the only man in Washington who could be used to knock Powell down, Clarence Mitchell of the NAACP, to the effect that the language could not touch the Montgomery boycott; Scott read it to the House two days later.

The general debate at last ran out late Tuesday, and the bill then lost another day in the ritual of Calendar Wednesday. There was a mild irony there, for Calendar Wednesday had originally been instituted to circumvent the Rules Committee by allowing committee chairmen to call directly to the floor their unreported bills. Usually it was ignored. This was the only instance in the 84th Congress in which the call of the committees was actually undertaken. At the head of the list was the Agriculture Committee, headed by a North Carolinian. The annual amendments to the Agriculture Trade Development and Assistance Act were debated for three and a half hours and passed before the House went home to supper.

## Amendments and a Defection

Thursday's work began with a motion by Howard Smith to table the bill. It failed, 104 to 190, but the roll call wasted the usual half hour. And then the flood of amendments descended. Some were frivolous, some were splenetic, some were genuinely useful. Dies artfully introduced a very long series of procedural restrictions on the Commission's investigations. He explained, with satisfaction, that they were verbatim the safeguards that Celler himself had attempted, at one point, to apply to the Un-American Activities Committee while Dies was its Chairman. Dies read the roll of the liberal organizations that had supported them then. When another member criticized a word, Dies replied, "No, I think the rules, as I have offered them, are perfect. I would not want them weakened. I think they have been considered so long over so many years and my friend, Mr. Celler, has fought so valiantly for them that I have introduced them exactly the way he wrote them." Celler observed that Dies had never seen the virtue of them while he was running the Un-American Activities Committee, and concluded, "I think redemption has come a little late to the gentleman from Texas." But Keating said, "What's sauce for the goose is sauce for the gander," and the rules were written into the bill on a voice vote.

Another Texas member, John Dowdy of Athens, proposed

an amendment requiring that the commission also study discrimination on grounds of age. "On behalf of the liberals, I accept," Dies replied, tongue-in-cheek.

Many of the amendments were introduced to confuse the issue, like the right-to-work amendment, or to harass the bill's sponsors, like the proposal to have the Commission study discrimination against women. Celler batted them down, one by one, without emotion, reminding the House occasionally that the amendments were merely to kill the bill.

The pedestrian tone of the proceedings was broken, late in the afternoon, when William E. Miller of Lockport, New York suddenly delivered a vituperative assault on the bill. Miller, a Republican and an insider in the Party structure, five years later would become its national Chairman. At this time, he was a member of the Judiciary Committee and, most remarkable of all, he had sponsored the administration's bills in April. Now he moved to strike the enacting clause, declaring: "This legislation in its present form will destroy more civil liberties and civil rights than it will ever protect." He had been an assistant prosecutor at the Nuremberg trials and, he asserted, he was in a position to say that Hitler had imposed his control on Germany "by decree after decree, just like this piece of legislation."[58]

The minority leader, Joseph W. Martin of North Attleboro, Massachusetts immediately recognized the value to the South of this defection, and its danger to the Republican Party. "I want to talk to those of you on the Republican side of the House," Martin said, "because he [Miller] has put us in a position where the ultimate result could be great. I want to tell the Republicans in this House if they follow the Southern Democracy in the defeat of this bill, they will seriously regret it."

The South immediately made the most of the windfall that Miller had given them, and compounded it by quoting Martin. Miller's change of heart was fulsomely praised by one South-

[58] *CR*, 13562 C to 13563 A.

ern speaker after another as an act of unprecedented political heroism, a triumph of conscience over Party pressure. The evidence of the pressure was Martin's candid warning. On July 21 the *Richmond Times-Dispatch* commented, "A more blatant admission that the GOP is behind this vicious invasion of the rights of states for purely political reasons would be hard to imagine."

The Miller episode appeared to offer an example of the manner in which one bill's fortunes could affect those of another, entirely unrelated in its subject. The development of hydroelectric power generation at Niagara Falls had been for some years a matter of dispute in New York politics. By midsummer of 1956 only the House Rules Committee stood in the way of final passage of Senator Herbert Lehman's bill for public development. It had already been passed by the Senate and had been reported by the House Public Works Committee. Speaker Rayburn was urging the Rules Committee to act. Chairman Smith had so far refused, but Smith had the deciding vote in his Committee, and he was reported to be weakening. Miller was vehemently opposed to the Lehman bill. His district included the Niagara site, and he was the author of a bill for the private development of power there. Columnist Drew Pearson alleged that Smith, upon learning that Miller was about to change his mind on civil rights, let it be known that he was ready to return the favor.[59] Miller attacked this version as an "unconscionable lie." But the force of his denial was somewhat attenuated when he acknowledged that he had given advance notice of his defection to another Southern Democrat, Tic Forrester. Whatever the reason for it, Smith held fast, and the Lehman bill died in the Rules Committee on July 27.

## Smith Agrees to a Compromise

The Miller episode gave the South ammunition, but it hardly affected the balance of forces in the House, heavily

[59] *Post*, July 26.

in favor of the bill, or altered the strategies that derived from it. Both sides had maneuvered with restraint. The House leadership, in effect the Speaker, had eschewed any attempt to wear down the South in the all-night sessions that the Southerners had almost expected. On the other hand, adjournment was only a week or so away. The South knew that the leadership was under rising pressure to handle other legislation and would meet any overt attempt at filibuster with a cloture motion, for which it obviously had the votes. Cloture in the House required only a simple majority. As he had done in the Rules Committee, Smith now calculated shrewdly the moment in which to execute a graceful retreat that could win still another measure of delay.

As the House convened on Friday, July 20, Smith said: "I am going to suggest that we proceed with more celerity from now on than we have. I have had some discussions with the leadership, which I take the floor now to verify. . . ." The agreement was to limit amendments to Friday afternoon, but to withhold the final vote on the bill until the following Monday. Smith obtained public acknowledgment of the compromise from Celler and the two floor leaders, Martin and John W. McCormack.[60] By the end of the day the number of amendments proposed had risen to thirty. Some of them, on points of procedure, were accepted. Those that attacked the substance of the bill were defeated or ruled out of order. A good many were introduced merely *pro forma*, to give their sponsors a brief opportunity to make speeches for their constituents' ears, and then withdraw. The day finally ended, and the Saturday session was devoted to other business.

## Who Understood the Debates?

The debates had analyzed the civil rights bill clearly and thoroughly. But only a handful of people had followed the debates. During most of the four days, fewer than thirty

[60] *CR*, 13724-25.

members were on the floor. Many of those were simply waiting for their turns to deliver prepared speeches for the *Record*. It would be a generous estimate to say that, by the time the bill was passed, there were two dozen people in the whole congressional apparatus, counting not only members but staff, who thoroughly understood the bill and its implications as they had been illuminated by the debates.

Congress characteristically leaves the details of any bill to a small number of experts. The vast majority of votes are cast only on broad issues of principle, in this case the extension of civil rights enforcement versus the tradition of congressional inactivity. The circle of experts was particularly narrow in this instance, where the substance of the bill dealt in an extremely subtle and legalistic fashion with an unfamiliar body of law.

Certainly no one could have grasped the full significance of the debates from reading the newspapers. The press did a generally poor job of covering the bill's progress. This is not to say that the reporters themselves performed badly. The Washington press as an institution was not organized to cover this kind of debate thoroughly. Newspaper space and reporters' time were not made available for the massive job of representing the import of the debates. The bill had been introduced amidst a general consensus of politicians and editors that it would never pass. Everything that subsequently happened only confirmed that judgment. Because it was merely another foredoomed civil rights effort, its trials were never better than a second-rate story. Even in Washington politics, it was outranked by many events of clearly greater immediate significance. The President's illness, the dramatics of the struggle for the Democratic nomination, and the passage of other bills all overshadowed it. There was far more at stake, for instance, in the fight over the mutual security appropriation, that recurrent symbol of America's responsibilities abroad. The civil rights bill was considered by the entire press to be significant only as a gesture and an element in the jockeying between the two parties for advantage in the urban constituencies.

In covering a congressional story, the men of the intensely competitive press are typically diverted from today's events by the necessity of discovering accurately the direction of tomorrow's developments. A reporter cannot spend eight consecutive hours in the press gallery following the intricacies of the lawyerish exchanges. He moves from the galleries to the protagonists' offices, to the lobbies, asking what will happen next. Politics is carried on between adversaries, and the news of it lies in the drama of conflict. The reporter wants to know who is winning, and why. He is diverted, almost necessarily, from the substance of the conflict to the pure politics of it, to the procedural tactics by which it is to be carried forward. A reporter does not have time to read the thousands of pages of testimony and argument that comprise the full record of a civil rights bill. In any case, civil rights was, in 1956, only one of the many issues that each reporter was concurrently following.

The newspaper summaries of the bill itself were inaccurate as often as not, even in the most reputable newspapers. The original Justice Department press release was technically accurate, but far too compressed and general to give even a sophisticated reader any idea of the full scope of the bill. The correspondents were then required to reduce this description still further to a matter of one sentence for each of the bill's four parts. Parts III and IV could not be described in one sentence. The bill's implications were lost in the pyramiding of generalizations drawn from generalizations.

Among the newspapers commonly circulated in the Capitol, only the *Richmond Times-Dispatch* reprinted the Attorney General's full description of the bills. The *Times-Dispatch* was not widely read except among the Southerners. It was known in Washington chiefly as the voice of the Virginia Democratic organization, the Byrd machine, which was then the intellectual leader of the South in the resistance to school integration. The South's newspapers suffered the same disqualification as the South's politicians. They had all cried wolf too often. Their attacks on civil rights legislation had so frequently been specious and exaggerated that the reporters serving every other part of the country had learned to discount them heavily. Where its spokesmen were quoted, their complaints, too, were summarized and generalized to a point at which they lost their trenchant quality. It was the emotional perorations that were printed, not the taut legal arguments.

Frank Van der Linden, Washington correspondent for the *Times-Dispatch* and a number of other Southern papers, was probably following the debates more closely than any other reporter. He was in closer touch with the Southern leaders than anyone else writing for a major newspaper. Yet even he gave vastly more attention to a piece of pure rhetoric like the orotund Second Manifesto than he did to the hard information that the debates developed. In retrospect, it appears that the most important statement made on the floor was Celler's concession that the bill would permit federal authorities to bring school suits. Van der Linden was alone among the correspondents, as far as the author has been able to discover, to report this fact. And even he gave that news no better place than the third paragraph of a story that led with Howard Smith's concession of the obvious fact that the House would pass the bill. Even the *Times-Dispatch*, with its consuming interest in the issue, considered the debates less important than Richmond's slow movement toward a decision to attempt to stave off school desegregation through state legislation.

The failure of the press, and particularly of the leading New York and Washington papers, to cover the debates adequately meant not only that the country at large, but Congress itself, generally missed the substance of the long argument. The newspapers are an essential part of the delicate and largely informal communications network that keeps congressmen and senators in touch with developments outside their own areas of special interest. Not only congressmen but their staffs very rarely have the leisure to read the *Congressional Record* at random. When the newspapers fail to report the existence of a question, most members have no way to hear of it. That was particularly true in the midsummer of 1956, when every member's attention was divided among (1) his attempts to tend to his own bills in the chaos of the session's last days, (2) the elections in his own district, and (3) the turmoil generated by the coming conventions. It was not only possible, but almost inevitable, that only the small number of specialists who had sat through the civil rights debate of 1956 would remember its substance in 1957.

The House convened at noon on Monday, July 23. It passed the bill, 276 to 126, amidst uncontested predictions that it would never reach the Senate floor.

## The Situation in the Senate

In the Senate, a small group of men deeply committed to the cause of civil rights decided to make a determined effort, at whatever cost, to force a vote on an issue that, in their view, involved a moral imperative outweighing any practical considerations for another postponement. Hennings of Missouri, Lehman of New York, and Douglas of Illinois were the leaders of this drive and, in the end, virtually its only supporters. To the Senate leadership these three men's insistence on a vote represented merely an irritating and utterly unreasonable waste of time and, in fact, an irresponsible attempt to disrupt the orderly accomplishment of national business that absolutely had to be dispatched quickly.

The Senate intransigents decided to catch the bill immediately upon its arrival in the Senate chamber, and enter an objection to the routine referral to Eastland's Judiciary Committee. They hoped in this fashion to hold it on the calendar, from which it could be called directly for a vote. The Senate met at midday and began droning through its routine morning hour while the House was passing the bill. Most of the senators were at lunch. The intransigents had left Douglas on the floor as their sentry.

As time passed, Douglas grew increasingly apprehensive. The morning hour ended, and Senator Mike Mansfield embarked upon a long foreign policy speech. Douglas decided to go over to the House to see what was delaying the bill. He asked a House reading clerk where the bill was. The clerk hemmed and hawed, shuffling his papers and saying that he couldn't find it. Finally a Northern congressman saw Douglas and warned him that the bill had already been passed. Douglas rushed back to the Senate chamber to discover that he was too late. The House passage had been a tedious affair, with the full ritual of a recorded quorum call, then a negative roll call on recommitting the bill, then at last a positive roll call on passage. As Douglas had started southward, from the Senate to the House, through the labyrinthine corridors of the Capitol, the bill, in the hands of Joe Bartlett, a House reading clerk, had started northward toward the Senate. They missed each other in passage. The bill arrived in the Senate to find Lister Hill of Alabama in the chair and no one present to object to its routine referral to the Judiciary Committee.

Filled with chagrin, Douglas cast about for another opportunity to force the issue. When the majority leader, Lyndon B. Johnson of Texas, called up the foreign aid bill, Douglas demanded a quorum call and then rescinded it. Johnson, perceiving that Douglas intended to challenge him, bridled and immediately repeated the order for a quorum call. Only 29 senators answered, fewer than a quorum. At once Johnson moved a recess until the next morning. Douglas objected. Johnson coldly explained to him that a motion to recess was not subject to objection. It was a majority question, and a majority of the few senators present voted with Johnson. That ended Monday's proceedings, and it was already clear that the leadership intended to reach final adjournment by the end of that week.

## The Strategy of Each Side

The Douglas group was still desperately interested in obtaining a vote directly on the question of civil rights legislation. There were a number of ways to do it; most likely was the introduction of a motion to discharge the Judiciary Committee. Many senators who were totally reluctant to provoke a filibuster at that stage of the session would, willy-nilly, have to vote for civil rights in an election year. Conversely, the Senate leaders wished to avoid any vote at all if possible, and, if it were not possible, then they wanted to defeat Douglas on such an arcane point of procedure that the connection with civil rights would be obscured.

House procedure is simplicity itself in comparison with the Senate's. It is correct to say that the Senate is able to accomplish its annual labors only by a system of unanimous agreements to disregard its rules. Liberals have repeatedly complained that the Senate's rules are designed specifically to impede liberal legislation and, in particular, civil rights bills.[61] That exaggeration ignores the history of the Senate. Like any system of law, the rules enforce tradition, they provide leaders with more power than followers, and they give a decided advantage in every combat to those who trouble to familiarize themselves with the system. The Senate liberals had almost a tradition of disdain for the rules. They usually appeared to regard them as part of the apparatus of the enemy. In recent years only one of the liberals, Hubert Humphrey, had attained any notable competence in handling them. Johnson, on the other hand, was a consummate parliamentarian, and Russell of Georgia was another.

When the Senate convened Tuesday morning, it rapidly became apparent that the civil rights issue had been very deftly shut up in a tight box. Bills and motions can be freely

---

[61] For example, *CR*, 14326 A-B; for a further elaboration, see Howard E. Shuman, "Senate Rules and the Civil Rights Bill: A Case Study," *The American Political Science Review*, LI, No. 4, December, 1957.

introduced only in the morning hour that opens the Senate's day. But by merely recessing the previous night rather than adjourning, the Senate was technically continuing the previous day's business where it had left off. Even the simplest words are terms of art in the Senate, and a day runs precisely as long as the Senate means it to. Each new day begins with a morning hour that occupies two hours of the early afternoon. But a new day begins only after an adjournment has ended the old day; if there is no new day, then the rules provide no morning hour. Although the calendar showed the date as July 24, the Senate was in fact still in the legislative day of July 16. And, as the Senate's President Pro Tempore, Walter George, explained it from the chair to Hennings, "In view of the fact that the Senate recessed yesterday, morning business is not in order except by unanimous consent."

Lehman asked if it were then correct to conclude that "during the remainder of this session, the same procedure can be invoked and one objection will forestall the presentation of any motions, the introduction of any bills, or the transaction of any part of the business of the Senate."

". . . there is no morning hour automatically, and a motion or bill can be presented to the Senate only by unanimous consent," George replied.[62]

Hennings asked unanimous consent to submit a discharge petition to wrest H.R. 627 from the grasp of Eastland's Judiciary Committee. But Russell objected. There was a good deal of complaint from the Douglas group, but, as Johnson and the Southerners patiently explained, the rules were the rules.

Lehman angrily asked Johnson whether, in his entire career, he could recall an occasion when the morning hour had been left at the mercy of a single objection.

"I have not done any research on the question," Johnson responded, adding:

[62] *CR*, 14161 A.

The majority leader is concerned with orderly process. The majority leader never attempts to program proposed legislation which has not been reported by a committee. The majority leader is confronted with a number of extremely important bills, such as the customs simplification bill, the Federal pay raise bill, the retirement bill, the Social Security bill, and any number of other bills, including bills affecting the farmers of the country. It was hoped that the Senate could act on all those bills and conference reports this week. The Senate has before it the very important mutual security appropriations bill. . . . The Senator from Texas feels that if we are to get into a hassle here, the Social Security bill may be endangered.

The Senator's selection of pending bills appeared to lean shrewdly toward the most heavily lobbied.

Hennings pointed out that the Senate was under no compulsion to adjourn that week. "None whatever," Johnson said. "If the Senator from Missouri is asking me a question, I will say we are not under any compulsion to adjourn by Saturday night, although I will say to the Senator I surmise the majority, who have it within their power to do so, would be willing and anxious, and perhaps eager, to conclude their deliberations in advance of the national convention."[63]

## Douglas Objects

At length, prodded by Russell, the Senate returned to the Mutual Security Bill. Twice in the next several hours Douglas broke in to ask unanimous consent to the introduction of his motion. Each time Russell objected. Douglas then lost his temper. Declaring that "two can play at that game," Douglas began to object to everyone else's routine requests. The atmosphere in the chamber became increasingly acid. Douglas blocked a bill of Humphrey's on Indian matters in Minnesota.

[63] CR, 14161 C to 14162 B.

Karl Mundt of South Dakota wanted to put into the *Congressional Record* an article on television, and Douglas objected. Glenn Beall of Maryland asked permission to extend his remarks. Douglas pondered the request, decided it did not constitute new business, and let it pass. Mundt sarcastically asked, "Mr. President, I should like to renew my request under the heading, 'Not New Business.'" Douglas doggedly objected again. Richard L. Neuberger of Oregon wanted to insert an article, and Douglas embarked on a series of hair-splitting questions; the presiding officer, John Stennis of Mississippi, cut them off with a ruling that they constituted an objection. The Senate was to recess at five o'clock for a reception for George, who was shortly to retire from the Senate. Douglas tried to force debate on the motion and was ruled out of order. When the Senate reconvened an hour later, Douglas read his discharge petition again, and again Russell objected. Douglas blocked a series of bills that John McClellan of Arkansas was trying to report from the Government Operations Committee, a committee report of Kefauver's on juvenile delinquency, and a bill from the Finance Committee.

Johnson bided his time with the patience of a cook waiting for his oven temperature to rise to the required heat. At length he said, "Mr. President, I should like to see how many members wish to have the Senator from Illinois continue the course he has followed today. Therefore I ask unanimous consent that, notwithstanding the order previously entered, the motion of the Senator from Illinois that the Senate stand in adjournment be held to be in order."

Technically the question was whether the Senate was to adjourn for a few minutes in the course of its day's work, but actually Johnson was challenging Douglas to demonstrate his support for a floor fight on the civil rights bill. The minority leader, Knowland of California, added:

> I wish to say that I concur wholeheartedly in the statement made by the majority leader. I think that either we are going to have orderly procedure in the Senate, or the procedure in

the Senate will be completely disrupted and the entire legislative program will be jeopardized. I consider that a vote against the motion of the Senator from Illinois will be a vote of confidence in the leadership of the Senate—not only the majority leadership, but the minority leadership as well.[64]

That was unusually forceful language and put the issue in a fashion that left most senators very little choice.

Douglas' motion was defeated by the humiliating vote of 6 to 76. The six were, predictably, Douglas, Hennings, Lehman, Irving Ives of New York, the erratic George H. Bender of Ohio, and William Langer of North Dakota, the last of the great "Sons of the Wild Jackass," who was always ready to vote against the leadership on any question. That devastating defeat made any further resistance useless. But when Robert S. Kerr of Oklahoma asked consent to report the Rivers and Harbors bill, Douglas again stepped in. "My head is bloody but unbowed," he said. "I must object."

At the end of the day, Hennings got the floor to deliver a denunciation of the administration's lack of support for its own bill. Knowland sharply rejoined:

The Senator knows as well as I do that under the conditions prevailing in the Senate such proposed legislation is not likely to be passed in the last four days of the Senate. The Senator from Missouri knows that, and I know it, and there is no need of attempting to kid either the American public, or a minority group, or the press.

## Who Knew What the Bill Contained?

Hennings' speech turned into a tirade against the Attorney General, a subject about which he had developed almost a monomania. The speech contained so much in defense of his own civil rights bills, and so much disparaging contrast of the administration's bill with his own, that it seemed less an

[64] CR, 14228 C.

advocacy of H.R. 627 than an indictment of Brownell for having failed to follow Hennings' drafts.

Hennings' performance included one very odd circumstance. He gave a description of H.R. 627 that covered only Parts I, II, and IV. It is impossible to know whether he skipped the broadest and most interesting section of the bill by accident or by design. In any event, the consequence was that the crucial Part III was never mentioned at all in the 1956 Senate discussions, which had little enough to say about the nature of the bill itself. Hennings alone among the liberals had followed it in Committee, and Hennings alone had a subcommittee staff to carry out the research on its language. Douglas had no precise idea of what the bill contained, and when it was introduced the following year, he was under the impression that it constituted an entirely new bill. He, like the other liberals, was fighting for a symbol. Hennings gave them no hint of the significance of this specific bill. His speech ended, Douglas complimented him, and the Senate recessed. Douglas, utterly cast down, not only by the magnitude of his defeat, but by the defection of most of his liberal friends, returned to his office and wept with chagrin.

The next day, Wednesday, Douglas decided not to let the defectors off so easily. He delivered a heated funeral oration for his lost cause.

> The Negroes of this nation are subjected, in many quarters, to great economic and physical pressure and are deprived of their basic rights under the Constitution. . . . I have probably not been very skillful in the efforts which I have made to bring this matter to a vote. I have tried my best but I know that on at least two occasions I have been outwitted by the very able field generals on the opposing side. I make no protestations of personal virtue. I believe we must seek to right the great wrongs we have inflicted upon the Negro people if we are to escape the judgment of a just God. I do not question the motives of those, however, who have taken a contrary position. I merely say this is an issue which will

weigh not only upon the conscience of the country, but upon the conscience of the Senate.

When Douglas charged that the Senate's temper and its procedures would prevent forever any civil rights legislation, Knowland mildly demurred. "To the contrary," he said, "I think it is quite possible to get civil rights proposed legislation before the Senate. . . . As I said to the Senator before, and as I say again, if I had the responsibility as majority leader, and my party was in control of the votes, as the Senator's party has been, I would endeavor to get a bill to the Senate early in the session, when the situation of a prolonged debate could be met, and not in the last four days."[65] In more guarded terms, Johnson made the same point.

On Thursday Johnson could easily afford to relent and permit adjournment. The next morning, knowing that the session would end that night, Douglas at last introduced his discharge motion. It was harmless, for the rules required it to lie over one day before it could be called up for a vote. "For how much longer," Douglas asked, "will the Senate and the country permit man-made rules to prevent us from even considering measures which the vast majority of the people desire?"[66]

Clifford P. Case of New Jersey replied, "This situation must not be repeated. We are determined to press at the next session of Congress for orderly but prompt consideration of the bill." He asked the two party leaders for pledges to effect early action on civil rights the following winter. Knowland said he hoped to see the legislation come to the floor "by March 1 or April 1 at the latest." But Johnson refused to commit himself, although Case pressed him hard.[67] There the matter rested.

Other liberals, in the course of the afternoon, showed their own distress at the fashion in which they had been trapped by

---

[65] *CR*, 14326 C.            [66] *CR*, 14937 C.
[67] *CR*, 15055 C to 15056 B.

circumstance. Neuberger and Humphrey took the floor to make the argument that Negroes had a substantial interest in the economic legislation that stood hostage to the liberals' good behavior. ". . . I believe that the Social Security bill contains more benefits for average families in this nation—families of any race, white or colored—than any other legislation of the 84th Congress or of recent years," Neuberger contended. "A man who has liberty but no economic security is in peril of losing his liberty too."

In the same vein, Humphrey added: "I could not in good conscience be part of a parliamentary tactic, the effect of which would be to hold the legislative process locked in its tracks at this crucial period before we had enacted a much-needed housing program . . . before we had enacted mutual security appropriations, farm credit extension and expansion, customs simplification, and scores of other legislative proposals which are so essential to the functioning of our democratic government."

Throughout the last three days of the session, the debate on civil rights kept sounding a familiar refrain: "Wait until next year."

The session was to end at midnight, and the evening wore on through a farrago of trivia. All the battles were over. And yet the civil rights bill came up once again when, just before the clock struck, Bender got the floor.

"Mr. President," he asked, "are we limited in any way?"

Vice President Nixon was in the chair. He glanced at the clock, which stood at 11.59 P.M., and replied, "To one minute."

"That is not enough," Bender began, and the Senate burst into laughter; some of that laughter must have been very wry indeed. "I have much to say about some of the uproar on civil rights," he declaimed. The responsibility for the bill's fate lay, he said, with the Democratic majority. Johnson asked him what the Republicans had done to pass a bill when they were in the majority. "I did everything I could," Bender hotly replied. "But I do not control the committee of which I am a member, and I do not like this demagoguery [more laughter] at the last minute on the part of the majority membership, trying to create the impression that somehow or other the Republican side is responsible for the civil rights program not becoming effective. . . ."

Spessard Holland of Florida broke in on a point of order to observe that it was now midnight. "The point of order is well taken," Nixon agreed. "The hour of twelve midnight having arrived, the Senate, in accordance with the terms of House Concurrent Resolution 276, stands adjourned sine die."

# ( III )

# The Campaign of 1956

LONG BEFORE THE CONGRESSIONAL SESSION ended, the partisans of civil rights legislation had begun to swing their attention to the nominating conventions. In May a series of labor union resolutions had called upon the parties to adopt unequivocal platforms. In June several states' Democratic conventions demanded a strong statement at Chicago.[1] And there was the customary Newtonian reaction, equal and opposite, from the Governor of South Carolina, George Bell Timmerman, who arrived at the annual Governors' Conference on June 24 to propose that the Southern states attempt to cause a tie and throw the presidential election into the House of Representatives.

But in Washington, Democrats of all persuasions were talking about a negotiated compromise of their differences. Senator Douglas, dispirited after his defeat in Congress, said that he would lead no civil rights campaign in the convention. Paul Butler, the Chairman of the Party, hopefully prophesied that the convention would peacefully accept its Platform Committee's draft on civil rights and that perhaps there would not even be a minority report.

[1] For example, the International Ladies' Garment Workers Union convention, May 13; AFL-CIO convention, May 14; Amalgamated Clothing Workers Union convention, May 22; Michigan Democratic convention, June 2; Wisconsin Democratic convention, June 17; New York Democratic convention, June 19.

The Party's leadership was deeply impressed with the necessity of deft and tactful handling of the issue throughout the campaign. Stevenson had lost four of the eleven Southern states in 1952, and in 1956 it was difficult to see how he could become President without recapturing them. Butler extended the honor of delivering the convention's keynote address to Frank G. Clement, the young Governor of Tennessee.

Reciprocally, most of the senior Southern politicians, and particularly those who knew Washington, were under no illusions about the price that they would pay if the Democratic candidate were beaten through a third party split. They proceeded with great efficiency to bring their hotspur segregationists under control. Timmerman had been talking loudly about an alternative for the South in the event that the convention turned out badly for it. He had set up a meeting of Democratic chairmen from the Southern states at Atlanta, as it happened, the day after the Second Manifesto of defiance was presented to the House of Representatives. The Atlanta meeting adjourned with a firm agreement that there was to be no thought of a third party. Three weeks later a larger convocation of Democratic leaders was held, again in Atlanta, this time with some of the senators on hand. John Sparkman of Alabama, a powerful Stevenson supporter and his running mate in 1952, was chosen chairman of the Southerners' committee on convention tactics. Its announced purpose was to achieve a "moderate" plank on civil rights "in a spirit of loyalty" to the Party.

## The Civil Rights Plank in the Democratic Platform

Other than the choice of candidates, the Party's ancient dispute over the Negro was the only matter of substance before the convention. It seemed so well under control by the second week of August that the convention's managers took the risk of rescheduling the Platform Committee's civil rights statement into an evening session in order that the largest

possible television audience could appreciate the Party's
unanimity of spirit. No sooner had they done so than Stevenson, with one casual remark to a television reporter on
August 7, shook the whole unsteady framework of the truce
they had patched together.

Stevenson had just emerged from a long conversation with
correspondents gathering for the convention. Under an
agreement that he was not to be quoted, he had discussed his
intentions with great candor. As he stepped out of the meeting
he encountered the television man, who asked him the question about which he had just been talking at length. Openly
and apparently on the spur of the moment, Stevenson said
publicly what he had been saying privately. The party leaders
were appalled and the Southerners full of wrath. The Southern delegates held a caucus on August 8 and threatened to
abandon Stevenson.

What Stevenson had said was that the Democrats faced an
obligation to write a platform on civil rights stronger than
that of 1952, and to declare their support for the Supreme
Court's desegregation decisions. The Southerners hoped to
hold the parties to a reiteration of earlier platforms predating
the school desegregation decisions. Northern liberals wanted
to extract endorsements of those decisions. Having not very
much else to fight over, the conventions fought all the harder
over platform language on civil rights.

On Wednesday of the week before the Democratic convention, Representative John W. McCormack, the Chairman of
the Platform Committee, announced his Subcommittee on
Civil Rights. McCormack himself was to preside over it. The
fourteen other members were the usual mixture of liberal and
conservative, Negro and Southerner, Stevenson backer and
Harriman backer. But most of them had one characteristic in
common: they got along well with the two Texans who were
the Democratic leaders in Congress. And the two Texans
were working diligently to avoid the open row that could
benefit only Harriman. McCormack himself was Speaker

Rayburn's majority leader. The Negro was Dawson. The Southerners included former Governor John Battle of Virginia, a staunch Stevenson man; Senator Sam Ervin, who had been at the Atlanta meeting; and Representative Brooks Hays of Little Rock, Arkansas, the model of the Southern moderate. The representative of the Harriman camp was a not very prominent lady from Oklahoma.

On Thursday Harry Truman arrived in town. He promptly enlisted in the compromise movement. At a press conference he declared that the convention could very well settle for the 1948 or 1952 civil rights statements. Testifying before McCormack's Committee, he endorsed in principle the assertion of equal rights for minorities, but he argued that any mention of the desegregation decisions would cost the election. His display of restraint was particularly remarkable in view of his suspected partiality to Harriman. "I was very much surprised by Mr. Truman's sensible approach," said Battle with relief.

## The Implications for Harriman's Effort

Harriman continued to urge the convention to vote an explicit endorsement of the decisions. But on Friday the liberal members of McCormack's Platform Committee began circulating a draft for a civil rights statement in a much more cautious vein. It declared that "every American child irregardless of race or national origin, economic status or place of residence has full rights under the law without discrimination to every educational opportunity to develop his potentialities." Otherwise the draft was very similar to the 1952 platform.

This language was met with vehement condemnation by the intransigent element among the liberals. Their spirits rose sharply on Saturday, when Truman announced his support of Harriman for the nomination. On the same day Johnson declared himself a "serious candidate." The effect of Johnson's candidacy was to strengthen the compromise against the very dangerous possibility that Truman had created. It had seemed clear for weeks that Harriman's only real chance lay in an open battle, on the convention floor, over civil rights. Truman's support might encourage Harriman to grasp at that chance, the Party leaders feared. By becoming a candidate, Johnson had not only strengthened his hold over the delegates he controlled, but had posted a warning to Stevenson not to attempt emulating Harriman. The Southern delegates now had a wider choice of candidates.

## The Position of the Liberal Democrats

Three hundred liberals, most of them delegates, met in the Morrison Hotel on Sunday to lay plans for a challenge from the floor. Roy Wilkins presided, and both Lehman and Walter Reuther, the President of the United Automobile Workers, spoke. But on that same afternoon Mrs. Franklin Delano Roosevelt arrived in Chicago to lend her support to the compromise. To the liberal Democrats, Mrs. Roosevelt was, more than any other person in the country, the authentic keeper of the New Deal tradition. For nearly a generation she had given effective and courageous support to the campaign for Negroes' rights. If she now said that it was time to compromise, there were not many people in the Party who found it easy to contradict her. When the convention opened on Monday, she urged it to approach the question with "imagination and understanding." The convention also heard that other representative of conscience, Paul Douglas, speak not only for civil rights but for Party unity as well. And while they spoke, Johnson, putting his faith in private conversations rather than public oratory, worked among the delegates.

Precisely because Stevenson himself was against the compromise, it was possible for other liberals to be for both the compromise and Stevenson. Because he had declared himself for explicit citation of the desegregation decisions, his supporters could argue that the Party already had, in the personal philosophy of the likely nominee, a far more binding assurance of future policy than any platform could provide, and tact in wording the platform merely increased the possibility that his policy would be given effect through a Democratic victory. When liberal leaders like Mrs. Roosevelt endorsed the compromise, then liberal followers by the hundreds were protected in voting for it.

But the most inflexible of civil rights proponents remained suspicious of Stevenson's intentions, thanks to the labors of Kefauver and Harriman. They wished to admonish him by getting approval for a strong civil rights plank from the several thousand men and women who ran the organizations upon which his campaign relied. The symbolic citation was, more broadly, essential to all those who had fought for civil rights legislation, had been beaten in Congress, and hoped to fight again. They wanted to show that the convention, with its fair approximation of majority rule, would return a different result from the adamant refusals of Congress with its intricate procedures, its seniority system, and its Southern leadership.

The Civil Rights Subcommittee met Tuesday night and well into Wednesday morning, working out the final language of the compromise. It was finally voted out unanimously but for the five *pro forma* negatives of the Southerners, who certainly had no real intention of impeding it. Even the Harriman lady from Oklahoma went along with it. The liberal dissenters immediately began looking for the support they required to challenge it on the floor. They needed eleven signatures on the minority draft to bring it before the convention, and the majority of the delegates in eight delegations to force a roll call vote. By the time the Wednesday evening session opened, they had fourteen signatures,[2] and the Chairman of the Michigan delegation had formally requested recognition, on their behalf, to move a roll call.[3]

[2] C. A. H. Thomson and F. M. Shattuck, *The 1956 Presidential Campaign* (Washington: The Brookings Institution, 1960), pp. 145-146.
[3] R. Bendiner, "Compromise on Civil Rights—I," *Reporter*, Sept. 6, 1956.

The majority and minority drafts differed in only one respect. The majority draft pledged the Party, in general terms, to end illegal racial discrimination. The minority would have committed the Party specifically to enforce the Supreme Court's desegregation decisions. Intense negotiations opened promptly, as Butler and other party leaders tried to talk the dissenters out of their crusade. The dissenting movement was now under the leadership of Lehman, Robert Short, Chairman of the Minnesota delegation, Governor G. Mennen Williams of Michigan, and Paul Douglas, who had reconsidered his earlier pacifism now that a battle was actually in prospect.

## Conversations Behind the Rostrum

The attempt at reconciliation proceeded under the most urgent pressure of time. The platform was to be adopted that night. The conversations continued heatedly in Butler's office, directly behind the convention's rostrum. The dissidents were unwilling to recede on any point. Butler endeavored to talk the Southerners into accepting stiffer language on peripheral matters and discovered them to be equally firm. On the other side of the curtain, in front of the delegates and the television cameras, the less incendiary sections of the platform were read as slowly as possible in the hope that the fight, if it came, might be so late that the smallest possible television audience would enjoy it. The bands played football songs. The delegates cheered vacuously. The news commentators interviewed each other.

The discussions got nowhere. Finally, after midnight, McCormack stepped before the convention, read the majority draft, and moved its adoption. Short read the minority draft. And, last of all, Harry Truman came forward to the microphones, to the surprise of his listeners. Ever since he had arrived in Chicago there had been a patent inconsistency between his endorsement of a civil rights compromise and his support of Harriman. Now, in this moment of emergency, he resolved it with a resounding call for Party unity. Asserting that he himself had done more to effect minorities' rights than any other President, he called the majority draft the best civil rights platform in the Party's history. If the dissidents had ever had any chance of success, it vanished in that moment.

Speaker Rayburn, Chairman of the convention, called for the ayes and the noes on the minority draft. There were two great roars, and in the opinion of the chair the noes had it. Then he asked for the ayes and the noes for the majority draft. In the opinion of the chair, this time the ayes had it. Across the floor of the hall, here and there standards were waggled to demand a roll call. Harriman's New Yorkers waved their standard vigorously, and so did the Georgians, who wanted a record of their intransigence.

"No, no, now just a minute," Rayburn said. "I have taken the ayes and the noes many times, and I think I can tell." The Michigan delegation, which had been promised recognition at this point, inexplicably declined to claim it. Presumably the Stevensonians had been at work among the Michiganders. And for the rest, the demands for the floor were half-hearted gestures that were not taken seriously because they were not meant to be taken seriously. At the showdown there were not very many delegates willing to press the issue at the cost of disrupting the convention. Dawson, a Negro who had supported the compromise, came forward to deliver a mild justification of it, and at 1.41 A.M. the convention was adjourned. At two o'clock one of Harriman's managers conceded that he now had no further chance of nomination.

That evening Stevenson was nominated on the first ballot, and the following evening he was given Kefauver for a running mate. "With leadership," the candidate said, "we can rekindle the spirit of liberty emblazoned in the Bill of Rights. We can build this new America where the doors of opportunity are open equally to all—the doors of our factories and our schoolrooms."

## The Republican Convention Faces a Similar Problem

The Republican convention the following week in San Francisco went through a rather similar exercise to arrive at approximately the same posture. The two parties differed greatly in political style. The Republicans were on top and believed that with Eisenhower they were likely to remain there. The Republican Party covered a narrower distance between its extremes, and it did not share the Democrats' traditional passion for internecine combat. Disputes within the Party were particularly muted in 1956 because the Party's candidate was the incumbent President, and its public stance inevitably was dominated by the President's personal views. And yet the issue cast up to the Republicans was the same as that with which the Democrats had been forced to wrestle.

One of the peculiarities of the campaign was the general assumption, throughout the country and among the Republicans' chief strategists, that Eisenhower's political strength had been eroded, in the normal pattern, by his four years of responsibility and by his two grave illnesses. Because their Party was in the minority, Republican strategy in a presidential election had to be an attempt to alienate registered Democrats. The civil rights issue confronted the Republicans with the same difficult choice as it had the Democrats. The President had done unexpectedly well in the South four years before. Should the Republicans recruit Southern Democrats or Northern Democrats? The Southerners were likely to prove more congenial and, over the decades, a much more stable asset to the Party. But the Southern states' weight in the electoral college was not heavy. The really decisive power, in presidential politics, lay in the big industrial states of the Northeast and Far West. Republican alliances there would be volatile and hard to maintain, but the potential rewards could be enormous and immediate. Those who played for the long term at low risk looked to the South; those who played winner-take-all were much more interested in reawakening Negroes' loyalties to the party of the Emancipator. The difference was one of temperament.

## The President's Position

As a politician Eisenhower was, in all ways, *sui generis*. He refused to see the issue in the hard categorical terms so clear to the Party's professionals. At a news conference two weeks before the convention, Chalmers Roberts of the *Washington Post* tried to force him to choose between opposites. Would the President want his platform to endorse the desegregation decisions, or would he not? "I don't know, Mr. Roberts, how the Republican plank on this particular point is going to be stated," the President replied, "and I have not given any thought of my own as to whether it should just state it in that way." He could only point out, he added, that he was sworn to uphold the Constitution. Another questioner then asked whether the administration proposed to speed up desegregation. The President mildly replied that the Supreme Court had left that matter in the hands of the federal district courts. Where there was no progress, he thought the courts would take action.

Several ranking Republicans hopefully inferred that the President had not made up his mind. They set about staking out a party position forthrightly in favor of faster school desegregation. Senator Prescott Bush, Chairman of the Republican Platform Committee and a candidate for re-election in Connecticut, promptly called for specific endorsement of the Court decisions by the convention. Senator Dirksen, up for re-election in Illinois, was presiding over the Republican Platform Subcommittee on Civil Rights when the Democratic platform appeared. "An equivocal nothing," he jeered. Predicting that the Republicans, in contrast, would be "unequivocal," he declared that a decision of the Supreme Court "can't just go floating around in the air. If it has any meaning, it has to be enforced—and sooner or later you're going to have to say it." Leonard W. Hall, the Chairman of the Party, called the Democratic declaration "no more than a spider web," and he promised that the Republicans would stand on the Court decisions as the law of the land. Jacob Javits, Attorney General of New York and the Republican candidate for Lehman's seat in the Senate, was also in San Francisco, urging the Party to capitalize upon the Democrats' shortcomings. "We are the party most capable of unity on civil rights," he said, urging a declaration by the Party that United States attorneys must take the initiative in forcing the pace of desegregation.

## Phone Calls to Washington

But as these brave things were being said, a planeload of the President's advisers and assistants, among them Attorney General Brownell, left Washington to take the Platform Committee in hand. Over the weekend the gentlemen from Washington conferred at length with the Civil Rights Subcommittee. On Saturday, Senator Bush announced that the platform would have "nothing in it that could fairly offend the South." On Sunday, the Southern Republicans decided that, their previous threats to the contrary, they were not adamantly opposed to a declaration that the Supreme Court's decisions were the law of the land; they only objected to any promise that the law would be enforced.[4]

The ultimate issue lay, not between the Northerners and the Southerners, but between the Subcommittee in San Francisco and the President in Washington. The final language was worked out in a protracted evening session that revolved around a series of long-distance telephone calls. Most of the Subcommittee, and all of the Justice Department officials on the scene, were convinced that the campaign required a flat statement on Negroes' rights. But the President refused to

[4] *NYT*, Aug. 19, 20; *Post*, Aug. 20.

take a strong position. The Subcommittee repeatedly called the White House during the evening, trying to persuade the President to move a little closer to the powerful legislative program drafted by the Justice Department earlier that year. The President repeatedly refused. Finally the Committee was told that the President had gone to bed leaving a message that if the Republican Party did not like his position, the Republican Party could find another candidate.

The Platform Subcommittee's response was ingenious. On Monday morning, as the convention opened, it brought out its draft. "We support," it announced, "the enactment of the civil rights program already presented by the President to the Second Session of the 84th Congress."

In the President's view, the only program he had presented to Congress were the two mild bills requested in the formal letters to the Vice President and the Speaker on April 9, to establish another Assistant Attorney General and Civil Rights Commission. But neither the newspapers nor the country was aware of any distinction between those two bills and the two broad enforcement bills that had subsequently been sent to Congress by Brownell.

In an editorial, the *New York Times* bestowed solemn approval upon the Republicans for having "pledged themselves specifically to work for the enactment of the President's six point program. . . ." It had been a four-point program in the spring; the two additional points were evidently generated in a highly enthusiastic and repetitive explanation by the Platform Subcommittee to the *Times'* reporter. There were other newspapers, like the *Washington Post*, that noted, cautiously, the lack of any specific description of the program. But nowhere was there any hint of the profound difference that lay between the President and his Justice Department. Once again it had been successfully papered over. Knowledge of it was still limited to a small circle of ranking insiders.[5]

The platform went on to declare that "the Republican

[5] Proceedings of the 1956 Republican Convention, *NYT*, Aug. 22; *Post*, Aug. 21.

Party accepts the decision of the U.S. Supreme Court that racial discrimination in publicly supported schools must be progressively eliminated." In language closely parallel to the President's at his press conference, it agreed that the responsibility lay essentially with the local federal courts. But it concluded, "This progress must be encouraged and the work of the courts supported in every legal manner by all branches of the Federal Government to the end that every constitutional ideal of equality before the law, regardless of race, creed, or color, will be steadily achieved." That was a good deal farther than Eisenhower had ever gone, let alone the Democratic convention. Some of the activists, like Javits and former Governor Thomas E. Dewey of New York, made it clear that they were disappointed. But Wilkins of the NAACP and Joseph Rauh, President of Americans for Democratic Action, busy lobbying in San Francisco, put out a statement judging the Republican declaration on civil rights to be "a thin shade stronger" than the Democrats'.

In accepting the nomination, the President touched upon the issue again. In that speech and throughout the campaign, he continued to speak of Negroes' rights as though the federal responsibility were limited to the areas of direct federal jurisdiction. He cited the elimination of discrimination in the armed forces, the desegregation of public accommodations in the District of Columbia, the pressure on government contractors to hire Negroes. Nixon, on the other hand, reflected much more closely, as he usually did, the view of the Party managers. In one sweeping sentence, as he stood before the convention, he promised Negroes "equal opportunity to obtain proper housing, decent medical care, good education and the unlimited chance for employment, according to his ability, which is every American's right."

## Unplanned Events Affect the 1956 Campaign

The campaign of 1956 was not, as presidential campaigns go, a particularly significant one. Both of the candidates shared a profound distrust of the Party organizations that they respectively represented; perhaps that contributed to the elevation of their views, for both instinctively tended to resist the importunities of the Party professionals and the interests that pressed them. And yet no dialogue ever developed between the candidates. Eisenhower spoke only to the nation, and Stevenson only complained about Eisenhower. No new issues really reached the voters. Eisenhower never ventured onto new ground. When Stevenson tried it, with the nuclear testing issue, he seemed to disclose a disturbing inability to communicate intelligibly with the mass of American citizens. Eisenhower usually spoke to the specific circumstances at hand. Stevenson commanded a far wider vision, yet he seemed often to speak in terms so broad as to be vague in their application. It was always apparent that Stevenson felt very differently from Eisenhower, but it was never clear precisely what, as President, he would have done differently.

The campaign was dominated by events, in this country and abroad, that were totally unforeseen by the conventions. The two candidates were to a degree stunned by them. First, the nation was confronted with an unexpectedly violent reaction to desegregation in half a dozen small towns. And then open warfare broke out in Hungary and in Suez.

## Violent Reactions over School Desegregation Orders

By the summer of 1956, school desegregation suits had been filed in every Southern state except Mississippi. The courts, the Justice Department, and the NAACP permitted the cases in the Deep South to lie dormant while the battle was carried on actively through the great peripheral crescent that begins in Virginia, then turns through Kentucky and Tennessee into Arkansas, Oklahoma, and Texas. A dozen of these cases had actually resulted in the introduction of Negro children into previously entirely white classrooms. In half a dozen further cases, school officials had already announced their intention to comply with court orders.

The South was by no means unified in its response to the courts. In Virginia a weak Governor was being constrained by the Byrd organization to follow the line of greatest resistance. But in the Arkansas and Texas primaries desegregation had been largely a sleeping issue, and even in Tennessee it had turned out to be substantially less important than the politicians themselves had expected. In Kentucky, Governor A. B. Chandler declared, "Segregation is one of the things that must go." And Louisville, a city of 50,000 school children, one-fourth of whom were Negro, was preparing to abolish segregation at one great stroke when the schools opened that September.

But even in the states most inclined toward acquiescence, the balance between passion and reason was a narrow one. Particularly in those counties farthest removed from the sophistication and prosperity of the large cities, the court orders evoked a rough hostility that required only the merest invitation to burst out into an ugly tumult not very different from open rebellion.

## Riots in Clinton, Tennessee

Two days after Eisenhower was nominated, Frederick John Kasper arrived in Clinton, a small mining town in the hills of eastern Tennessee. Kasper, 26 years of age, had lately been a clerk in a Washington bookstore. But now he was Executive Secretary of the Seaboard White Citizens Council, and he immediately opened a door-to-door campaign in which he exhorted parents to picket their school. Clinton had been under a federal court order to admit Negro students to its high school, and when the term began on the following Monday, twelve of them were to join the 806 white students. Clinton High School was to be the first state-supported school in Tennessee to desegregate.

On Sunday afternoon Kasper was invited to sit down with a group of the town's leaders, who had been carefully shepherding Clinton toward peaceful acceptance of the judge's order. They asked Kasper to give up his crusade. He shrugged them off. He bore the evangelical message that under "common law" the people constitute a higher authority than the courts, and when the people speak, then the courts must recede. That night he held his first rally in front of the county courthouse. About fifty people turned up. The Assistant District Attorney General swore out a warrant for Kasper's arrest on a charge of vagrancy and inciting to riot, but he had to drop it for want of evidence.

On Monday,when the school opened, a news wire service distributed nationally a photograph of a slack-jawed adolescent picketing the school with a crude cardboard sign lettered: "Strike Against Intergration of Clinton Hi." On Tuesday night Kasper held another rally and drew a crowd of 500. Now he called for the resignation of the school's principal. On Wednesday he turned up at the school with a following of perhaps a hundred people. There the trouble started. Two boys were arrested. A fight flared up between a Negro and white man. The mob chased another Negro. Attendance at the school began to drop.

That night Kasper's speech at the courthouse had an audience of more than 1,200 people. While he spoke, a federal marshal unobtrusively served him with a warrant temporarily restraining him from interfering with the process of desegregation required by the court. Later that night, the men who had obtained the order drove to Knoxville, fifteen miles away, to ask Federal Judge Robert L. Taylor to hold Kasper in contempt. When morning came there was more fighting at the school, and the Negro pupils, now eleven, were taken out of the building under a shower of tomatoes and stones.

On Friday Judge Taylor found Kasper guilty of contempt of court and sentenced him to a year in prison. That night another agitator, Asa Carter of Birmingham, President of the

Northern Alabama White Citizens Councils, spoke to a crowd of perhaps a thousand at the courthouse and then hastily left town. The crowd, largely adolescent boys, began blocking traffic on U.S. 25, the main highway through town. They stopped Negroes' cars, rocked them, broke their glass, and flattened their tires. The town's six-man police force was powerless.

On Saturday morning Clinton's Mayor flew in a chartered plane to Nashville to ask Governor Clement for help. Clement promised both highway patrolmen and National Guardsmen.

The segregationists' rally was to begin at eight o'clock. A crowd of 2,000 accumulated. As they began to form a solid mass, the town police formed a skirmish line and broke them up with tear gas. And just at that point a large contingent of state highway patrolmen arrived. Under their eyes the rally proceeded uneasily but peacefully. It was something of a failure, the chief speaker, a Chattanooga judge, failing to appear.

The National Guard marched into Clinton on Sunday morning. There were 633 Tennessee Guardsmen, with three armored personnel carriers and seven M-41 tanks, under the command of State Adjutant General Joe W. Henry. The General issued orders prohibiting all outdoor assemblies in Clinton and all outdoor speeches, as well as parking or assembling in the courthouse square after six at night. The Constitution, it seemed, was suspended and, although no one used the term, the town was under a measure of martial law. Clinton fell quiet. Attendance at the high school dropped to 266.

What had happened in Clinton was serious enough. But the electric effect of the news coverage upon readers throughout the country even heightened the sense of crisis. Newspapers in every city printed the photographs of the tanks rolling through the town, small clusters of apprehensive townspeople in the background. The riflemen showed the grimly shadowed visages that helmeted men always wear in photographs.

Those who supported desegregation were gratified, those who opposed it were dismayed, and the whole nation was left to ponder the profound meanings of this encounter for the country's future.

Much the same thing happened a few days later in two western Kentucky villages, Sturgis and Clay. Governor Chandler met segregationist riots equally promptly with Guardsmen. With bayonets fixed, the soldiers charged the mob in Sturgis. The tanks, the Governor explained, were taken along "for the proper psychological effect"; as he put it, "No man is going to argue with a tank."

## The Justice Department Enters a Case

The newspapers' attention followed the tanks, and yet in other towns the strife over desegregation took other courses of greater meaning to the political issue as the federal government encountered it. The School Board of Hoxie, Arkansas had desegregated its classrooms a year before. Segregationist organizations had undertaken a campaign of harassment extending to a boycott so effective that at length the schools had to be closed for want of pupils. The School Board obtained a federal injunction against interference, and the schools reopened. The segregationists attacked the injunction. The State of Georgia entered the case as amicus curiae in support of them. The United States Department of Justice came forward as amicus in support of the School Board, the first time that the federal government had ever appeared in court to ask for implementation of the desegregation decisions. The Circuit Court of Appeals upheld the injunction, ruling, in effect, that a federal judge has the authority to protect a local board in carrying out his orders.

## Mobs in Texas

In two Texas towns the question was cast in a more portentous form. There the Governor chose to stand with the mob. Mansfield, Texas was under an injunction to desegregate, and the Court of Appeals had held that local opinion was not a sufficient reason for denying Negro children prompt admission. The town's few Negro children had been going to school in Fort Worth. When several of them tried to enroll at the local high school, a large and unruly crowd physically barred them from the school building. Governor Allen Shivvers telephoned Mansfield school officials to urge them to "transfer out of the district any scholastics, white or colored, whose attendance or attempts to attend Mansfield High School would be reasonably calculated to incite violence." The Governor said publicly, "It is not my intention to permit the use of state officers or troops to shoot down or intimidate Texas citizens who are making orderly protest against a situation instigated by the National Association for the Advancement of Colored People." At the school, Texas Rangers impassively stood by as a minister admonished the whites to "put the Bible's love thy neighbor together with this crowd." A voice shot back, "This ain't a love thy neighbor crowd." No Negroes appeared. The injunction remained in force, but the children named in it returned quietly to the Negro school in Fort Worth. They had won a technical victory in the courts, but against the power of the state they were unable to make use of it. And a week later Texas Rangers again stood by, watching, as a mob, jeering and flinging gravel, by violence prevented two Negro students from entering the Texarkana Junior College.

The lesson seemed clear. The state authorities could impose orderly desegregation upon school systems, even in the face of public violence. Federal lawyers could offer substantial help to a beleaguered local school board, even where the state remained passive. But where the Governor of a state openly promised immunity to the mob, the mob ruled.

Throughout that month of September, despite the news of rioting, the evidence of the Southern mood continued to be astonishingly mixed. The schools of Louisville opened completely desegregated with an almost total lack of protest.

And meanwhile the General Assembly of Virginia, in special session, was hotly passing legislation to cut off state funds to any local school district that desegregated. Apparently the principle of local determination of local policy, Richmond's shield against the federal government, was not to apply to Arlington County in its differences with Richmond. North Carolina's voters overwhelmingly approved a Constitutional amendment to permit their districts, by popular vote, to close their schools; and yet it seemed upon careful examination to be a device for keeping schools open, by returning the responsibility to the local level. At Lake Junaluska, North Carolina, the Ninth World Methodist Conference, at which delegates had been housed and fed without regard to race, declared: "The conference is entirely convinced that the church is committed by its very nature to the establishment of a human society in which discrimination based on race or color will no longer exist." The Baptist General Convention of Texas published a denunciation of racial violence and called upon all Christians to "show friendship and consideration for persons of all races with whom a person is associated."

## The Candidates Are Cautious

The candidates were cautious, understandably, in commenting upon the schools and the Negroes. "Let us remember this," the President said to his news conference. "Under the law the federal government cannot, on the ordinary case of keeping order and preventing rioting, cannot move into a state until the state is not able to handle the matter." When he was asked about Governor Shivers' support of the crowd, the President replied that he was unfamiliar with the facts of the situation, and in any event it was in the hands of the courts. Kefauver carefully said, at a news conference in Virginia, that he opposed the use of federal force to compel the integration of schools. "The states have shown they are competent to handle the situation," he explained. A month earlier the issue had been whether the Party platforms were to mention the desegregation decisions. Now the issue was whether the federal government must enforce them with troops.

Eisenhower seized gratefully upon the happy example of Louisville and its Superintendent of Schools, Omer Carmichael. "I read about this man Carmichael . . . ," said the President. "I think Mr. Carmichael must be a very wise man." Carmichael was invited to the White House shortly afterward and was photographed in conference with the President. Stevenson spoke of his "admiration for those citizens of Southern communities, and those governors, mayors and local officials, who are upholding the rule of law, sometimes even against their own personal feelings, sometimes in the face of violence. . . ."

Stevenson's campaign on civil rights got off to an unpromising start. He scheduled a major speech in Harlem, and the *New York Times* promptly reported that Democratic leaders were advising him against appearing there. The outbursts at Clinton and Sturgis, the *Times* explained, had inflamed Negro sensitivity upon the subject of desegregation and reminded the voters of the shortcomings of the Democratic platform.

A week later Stevenson began to attack Eisenhower directly on the racial issue. Addressing the leadership of New York's Liberal Party, Stevenson observed that the President had made no effort to induce national acceptance of desegregation. He had repeatedly refused to suggest any measure of personal support for the doctrine, Stevenson continued. At a news conference in early September Eisenhower had been asked whether he supported the decisions, or whether he merely accepted them. "I think it makes no difference whether or not I endorse it," the President had answered. "The Constitution is as the Supreme Court interprets it, and I must conform to that and do my best to see that it is carried out in this country." Stevenson assailed this tepid pas-

sivity. "I count it," he said, "the responsibility of the Chief
Executive to do all in his power to create a climate of compliance with the law, and to encourage with the immense
prestige and influence of his office those who are earnestly
trying, often in difficult circumstances, to comply with the
Court's decision." The principle was well stated, but Stevenson failed to put forward any specific recommendations for
the accomplishment of such a difficult duty. A week later, at
a news conference in Washington, Frank Van der Linden
asked Stevenson whether he approved of the handling of the
desegregation cases in Tennessee and Kentucky, and what
he would have done differently from Eisenhower. In reply
to the first question, Stevenson said that he approved the
Governors' prompt use of force to protect public order and
the processes of compliance with the courts. In reply to the
second question, he declined to answer because, he said, he
was not familiar with the facts of the cases.

As time passed, the sense of crisis diminished. The school
year progressed, and, each in its own way, the embattled
towns came to terms with history. As school attendance rose
in the Clinton High School, the Guardsmen were withdrawn
until, by the end of September, the atmosphere was compara-
tively normal and the principle of desegregation was established in Tennessee. In Kentucky, the same principle had been
so resoundingly affirmed at Louisville that the state authorities could afford to give Clay and Sturgis another year of
segregation. The state's legal officers conveniently found
that the Negro children had not properly fulfilled the procedures that must precede integration. The disappearance of
the rowdies and the tanks from the newspapers made it much
easier for the candidates to talk about the races and the
schools.

In a show of courage, Stevenson declared his support of
desegregation in a speech at Little Rock, and he was applauded
for it. When he finally went to Harlem in early October, he
was received with enthusiasm. He alluded to his own activity,

as Governor of Illinois, on behalf of minorities' rights. "Yet," he continued, "despite the progress we have made, the achievement of equality of rights and opportunities for all American citizens is still the great unfinished business before the United States." He concluded with a fine resounding verse from the fifth chapter of Amos: ". . . let justice run down as waters, and righteousness as a mighty stream." But where the prophet had been exact as to who were to be smitten for their transgressions and how, Stevenson offered Harlem only a restatement of his general support for integration. The President commented that the Democrats "believe, apparently, that the cause of civil rights can be advanced by a formula of much oratory and little performance. We have talked less—but we have acted with patience, human understanding, and with concern for the equal standing of all before the law."

## Negro Leaders Switch to Eisenhower

During the campaign several ranking Negro Democrats defected to Eisenhower, the most important of them being the flamboyant Powell. He emerged from a half hour's conversation with the President to announce his decision, motivated, he explained, by the President's prestige abroad, by his policy on civil rights, and by the snubs that Stevenson had allegedly bestowed upon Powell himself. Powell subsequently told his constituents that the President, during their conversation, had confessed that he favored the summary arrest and jailing of anyone who disobeyed a desegregation order. In spite of the utter implausibility of the statement, and the character of its source, Southern Democrats made much of it for a week until the White House staff was finally able to extract a retraction from Powell.[6]

The Republican managers, still underestimating the President's hold upon the voters, grew increasingly anxious to

[6] *NYT*, Oct. 12, 24, 27.

respond to the open opportunity offered them by the Northern Negroes. In a television speech in early October Nixon gave great emphasis to his thesis that "the moderate approach of President Eisenhower" would lead, surely and directly, to the abolition of all racial discrimination in American life. While Eisenhower had spoken of presidential responsibility in terms of the areas of immediate federal jurisdiction, Nixon and the Party worked throughout October to make it clear that they intended to attack racial disqualifications not only on Army posts and in the District of Columbia schools, but everywhere. Nixon developed the point in the strongest terms when he addressed the Alfred E. Smith Memorial Dinner in New York: "Most of us here will live to see the day when American boys and girls shall sit, side by side, at any school—public or private—with no regard paid to the color of their skin. Segregation, discrimination, and prejudice have no place in America."

Deftly, Nixon avoided any direct collision here with Eisenhower's firm views. He carefully added that the federal government could not alone bring about this welcome prospect; no law was better than the will of the people to obey it, and "that will must come from within us." As a forensic technique, prophecy was remarkably effective. It proposed no policy and it promised no action, but it stated a result and let each listener infer to his own taste the speaker's intention.

## The President Endorses Brownell's Full Program

Particularly in New York, the Republicans were meanwhile going after Senator Eastland hammer and tongs. A vote for any Democrat, Javits contended, was a vote to keep Eastland in control of the Judiciary Committee. The argument persuaded the *Amsterdam News*, a Negro newspaper in Manhattan, to announce its support of Javits early in October.

The American Civil Liberties Union had asked both candidates for statements and published them on October 15.

Stevenson's paragraph asserted that the President was obliged to use his "moral as well as legal authority to create an atmosphere in which the law of the land can be carried out in tranquillity and order." Eisenhower's reply was to recommend the enactment of the familiar four points: establishment of a Civil Rights Commission; creation of a civil rights division in the Justice Department; provision of federal authority to seek injunctive protection of voting rights; and authority for the Justice Department to seek "preventive relief" in the full range of civil rights enforcement. "This is the program of the Republican Party," the President declared, "and I will continue to work for it until the full and free exercise of rights and privileges for every United States citizen becomes real and meaningful."

For the civil rights endeavor, this statement was the most significant event of the 1956 presidential campaign. The *New York Times*, one of the very few newspapers to give it any attention at all, dismissed it as "the program the President sought . . . this year." But that was precisely the point. The President had never sought it. Brownell had sought it, and he had arranged for the introduction of the bills in direct violation of the explicit instructions of the White House.

Brownell's tactics had made it quite impossible for the President and the Party's congressional leaders to disavow the unauthorized bills publicly. The politicians who knew the truth, or suspected it, had their own reasons for keeping silent. The secret was never told. Press and public had continued for six months in the belief that the President supported all four bills. But it was only in the heat of the final weeks of the election campaign, at a moment when the Republican leadership considered the outcome to be hanging in the balance, that the President finally endorsed the Justice Department's program.

This statement was the point at which Eisenhower became committed to the enforcement provisions. In its consequences this declaration, passed by with so little attention, far outweighed the civil rights section of the Party platform, upon which so many hundreds of thousands of words had been poured out, or any of the President's meticulously reported speeches on the subject.

## Olney Acts on Negro Voting

Shortly before the statement appeared, Warren Olney III, Assistant Attorney General in charge of the Criminal Division, had testified before a Senate subcommittee that the Department was investigating the mass disfranchisement of voters in Louisiana and Georgia. The government was considering prosecution in places like Ouachita Parish, Louisiana, where 3,397 of 3,912 registered Negroes had been stricken from the rolls. Nine days after the statement, Olney wrote letters to the chairmen of the interested congressional committees in which he broadened the charge. "Disfranchisement of colored voters in going forward on a mass basis," he said, and he located the trouble in Alabama, Georgia, Louisiana, Mississippi, and North Carolina. Governor James Coleman of Mississippi angrily retorted, "On its face this is a political move designed to get votes from Northern Negroes."

Coleman was partly right. But Olney's specific purpose was to make a case for the voting legislation that had been drafted, under his own direction, in the Criminal Division. While the campaign was increasing the general pressure for civil rights legislation, the case for Brownell's program was being built up within the apparatus of the Republican administration.

The publication of the statement to the American Civil Liberties Union had no visible effect on the President. To the end of the campaign he reflected, in his own speeches, the views with which he had begun it. He made a last swing through the South shortly before the election and spoke three times in Florida and Virginia. He touched on civil rights only once, in Miami, and then merely to urge the resolution of racial disputes at the local and state levels. Stevenson, speaking to the Liberals in New York the next day, sourly observed that the President, on his Southern tour, "talked more about states' rights than civil rights. He didn't even mention the Supreme Court decision on desegregation, and we still don't know whether he endorses it or not."

## Hungary and Suez

By this time it made little difference what the candidates said. In the last week of October public attention was sharply distracted from the campaign by a double crisis in foreign policy. Trouble had been threatening ever since early summer at Suez, where the Egyptian government had taken the Canal from its private French and British owners. Suddenly a joint British and French invasion force descended upon Suez. The question of American reaction was one that ran the length and breadth of the Atlantic alliance. During the same period the Hungarian revolt began, inviting the United States to give substance to its brave words about the liberation of Eastern Europe. Once again events extraneous to the campaign swept down upon the candidates, taking them quite by surprise. Every newspaper in the country was following the fighting at Suez and Budapest with far greater concern than the coming election, and in some papers it was becoming positively difficult to locate the campaign news. It was in this atmosphere that the election was held.

## The Negro Vote and Civil Rights

The elections demonstrated that Eisenhower was stronger in 1956 than he had been in 1952, and no one was more surprised than his own managers. In the immediate aftermath of the election, politicians and political writers pondered the evidence of changing loyalties among the traditionally Democratic Negro voters of the urban North and, even more striking, of the urban South. The diminished Democratic pluralities in the Negro wards was the standard second-day story in papers throughout the country.

James Reston observed in the *New York Times* of November 8 that Eisenhower had cut into the Democrats' strength in Northern cities to a point at which he had almost eliminated their pluralities. The *Washington Post* reported that while Eisenhower had won relatively few Negro votes four years earlier, in 1956 "he won a majority of the Negro vote in a number of Northern cities and in all the Southern cities." In Baltimore, the *Sun* noted on November 8 that the Republican candidate for the Senate, the highly conservative John Marshall Butler, had carried most of the Negro sections of the city. And that, according to the Republican city chairman, was "something a Republican had not been able to accomplish for more than two decades." He attributed it directly to the civil rights issue. One of the city's ranking Negro leaders, Juanita Mitchell, the wife of the NAACP's Clarence Mitchell, had switched to Eisenhower during the campaign.

Edwin A. Lahey commented on November 8 in the *Chicago Daily News*, "The Democrats were all things to all men on the civil rights issue in the recent campaign." He reported an interesting contrast in Negro politicians' explanations of the movement in Negro voting. Dawson, the Democratic loyalist, attributed it to "the war situation," and to large Republican expenditures: "Civil rights had nothing to do with it." And then Lahey quoted the turncoat Powell to the contrary: "It should serve as a warning to Democratic bosses that no one controls the Negro vote."

It was reasonable to assume, as Dawson did, that Negroes were moved by the same considerations that induced Americans generally to give the Republicans a bigger majority in 1956 than in 1952. But that explanation alone would not suffice. The Negro swing was far heavier than that of the whole voting population, and clearly some other motive had been in play.

The Democrats, to their consternation, lost 25 of the nation's 36 largest cities, including traditional fortresses like Chicago, Baltimore, Memphis, and Jersey City. Negro voting was, of the many causes, the most easily identified. Richard Lyons of the *Washington Post* reviewed the results in 22 cities on November 18 and concluded: "In every city surveyed, President Eisenhower won a larger percentage of the Negro vote than he did in 1952." And further: "While Negro leaders gave various reasons for the change, the vote pattern indicated that the overriding issue was civil rights. . . ." In an editorial, the *Post* commented: "So long as [the Southerners'] influence remains dominant in the formation of Democratic party policy, the drift of Negroes to the Republican standard is likely to continue. Sometime soon the Democrats will have to choose between white supremacy and civil rights." Several of the liberal periodicals, notably *Look,* the *Reporter,* and the *New Republic,* drummed away on the same point, with a wealth of statistics and quotations from Negro politicians, throughout November and into December.

Certainly a very solid statistical base underlay the reproaches that the liberals threw up to the Democratic Party. In Powell's Harlem district, 88 percent Negro (in the census four years later), the Republicans had won 17 percent of the vote in 1952 but 34 percent in 1956. In Dawson's Chicago district, 92 percent Negro, the Republicans took 25 percent of the vote in 1952 and 36 percent in 1956. In the Negro wards of Atlanta and Richmond, Eisenhower's vote was more than 50 percentage points higher in 1956 than four years before. The Republicans won Tennessee by 5,781 votes, obviously fewer than the increment in the vote for Eisenhower among Negroes in Memphis alone.[7] Eisenhower carried six Southern and border states in 1952, eight in 1956.

Three days after the election, Senator Humphrey charged that the Democrats "are digging their own graves by inaction in the field of civil rights."

[7] Congressional District Data Book, Bureau of the Census, 1961; Thomson and Shattuck, pp. 352-53.